I0704138

PROTESTORS UNITED

ALTERNATIVE SOLUTIONS

EDMOND DANTES VONGEHR

Copyright © 2018 Edmond Dantes Vongehr
All rights reserved
First Edition

PAGE PUBLISHING, INC.
New York, NY

First originally published by Page Publishing, Inc. 2018

ISBN 978-1-64214-949-4 (Paperback)
ISBN 978-1-64214-950-0 (Digital)

Printed in the United States of America

Contents

The Declaration of Independence states when in the course of events, it becomes necessary for the people to dissolve the political bands which have connected them with another and to assume among the powers of the earth, the separate and equal station to which the laws of nature and God entitle them, a decent respect to opinions of mankind requires that they should declare the causes that impel them to the separation.

We hold these truths to be self-evident, that all men are created equal, that they are endowed by a Creator with certain unalienable rights, that among these are life, liberty, and the pursuit of happiness. That to secure these rights, governments are instituted among men, deriving their just powers from the consent of the governed, that whenever any form of government becomes destructive of these ends, it is the right of the people to alter or abolish it and to institute new government, laying its foundation on such principles and organizing its powers in such form, as to them shall seem most likely to affect their safety and happiness. Prudence, indeed, will dictate that governments long established should not be changed for light and transient causes; and accordingly all experience has shown that mankind is more disposed to suffer, while evils are sufferable, than to right themselves by abolishing the forms to which they are accustomed. But when a long train of abuses and usurpations, invariably pursuing invariably the same object, evinces a design to reduce them under absolute despotism, it is right, and it is their duty to throw off such government and to provide new guards for their future security. Such has been the patient sufferance of these colonies, and such is now the necessity that constrains them to alter their former systems of government.

The following pages were collected from letters to the editor of the local newspapers, as well as articles by national columnists—all pertaining to the political, economic, and social condition of the country. This book offers alternative answers and solutions for a functional governance of the people, for the people, and by the people on changes for a higher standard of living for all Americans, who are authorized by the Declaration of Independence, the Constitution, and the Bill of Rights—mostly the right to life, liberty, and the pursuit of happiness.

The reasons for this book follow:

1. Restructure the economy (7/29/12, Mike E. Miles)
2. Pool failure disappointing
3. Bank of New York settles Madoff case (150-year prison term)
4. Southern Oregon University hosts forum on hunger and homelessness
5. Greed is the threat (Wayne Richards)
6. Nothing will change (11/11/12)
7. Ranks of American poor rise to 49.7 million
8. County rate of homeless (11/15/12)
9. Problems are serious (3/4/12, Gordon De Vos)
10. Protesters bring homeless into focus (11/13/11)
11. Lead by example (2/19/12, Victor Rogers)
12. Occupy Washington (11/8/11)
13. Now we get hate TV? (11/8/11, Tom Smith)
14. Why I'm angry (3/30/12, David Hammond)
15. Where are all the forward thinkers? (11/11, Allan Lee Wattenberg)
16. Why Americans are in the streets (11/11, Bruce Barnes)
17. Justice for all (12/11, Sidney Stitt)
18. Big changes needed (4/09, E. D. Vongehr)
19. Occupiers are heroes (11/11, Cynthia Zavatski)
20. Dump the Greedy Old Party (11/17/11, Allan Joumet)
21. Make the cheaters pay (4/11, Jaelle Dragomir)
22. Scientific government is needed (Ed Vongehr)
23. The Divided States of America (2/11, Ed Vongehr)
24. Take the money out (4/12)
25. Why we need government (5/12, Hartley Anderson)
26. Where is compassion? (5/11, Ralph Bagley)
27. Ike would weep (11/12, Harry Freiberg)
28. Tax cuts don't equal growth (11/12, Mark Heritage)
29. Corporations and profit (10/11, Frank Long)
30. Now is the time (10/11, Ed Vongehr)
31. Journal's view is different (1/12, Marie Reeder)

68. Union is innocent (11/12, Eric Kees)
69. Stop blaming workers (11/12, Charles McHenry)
70. Give God a try (12/12, John Mark Matson)
71. Pogo was right (12/12, Robert Warren)
72. Shootings are a symptom (12/12, Linda Hackwell)

No. 1
Restructure the Economy

In Japan, the average CEO salary is 23 times that of the average hourly-wage worker. In the United States, it's 233 times, and was touring 77 times before the recession. In Germany, 50 percent of the corporation boards must consist of the workers. Germany rarely outsources work to other countries. In France, workers are mandated in guaranteed five weeks' paid vacation per year. My generation (baby boomers a.k.a. the "weed and greed generation"), through American capitalism, has destroyed the livelihood of our children and children's children by outsourcing jobs to other countries. To counter this economic treason, immediately these sanctions must be put into place. In all stores in the United States, the inventory must consist than 80 percent product made in USA. Textile is maybe imported United States, but all clothes and shoes must be assembled in the USA. Cars built in the USA must be made of 80 percent American-made parts. American capitalism, the federal government, as well as our outdated Constitution failed us. We need to look to South Africa to rewrite our Constitution, and to France, Germany, Canada, and Australia to restructure our repugnant economic system.

—Mike E. Miles, Medford

No. 2
Pool Failure Disappointing

I was very disappointed to see that the bond for the pools and Medford did not pass. I just got home from living in Germany for the last five years where we had six, yes six, modem pools within fifteen minutes from our house between two towns the size of Center Point—three of them were indoors. I voted yes 48m parents have a big in-ground pool and never mind the grandkids and never mind the grandkids coming over and swimming. Have we really just become so attached to a machine that we can't think beyond our front door? We can't look out and see the bigger picture and how this would help many, many people in the community? And not to mention Hawthorne Park in dire need of some kind of change.

—Erich Norum, Central Point

No. 3
Bank of New York Settles Madoff Case (150-Year Prison Term)

New York-A Bank of New York Mellon subsidiary will pay $210 million to settle claims it concealed red flags showing Bernard Madoff was running a massive Ponzi scheme. Due diligence by Ivy Asset Management revealed discrepancies in Madoff's stated investment strategy, according to a statement by New York attorney general Eric Schneiderman, who announced the settlement Tuesday. While Ivy steered clients to invest in Madoff, thereby collecting fees for itself, some at the firm had been generations about Madoff, the attorney general said. Schneiderman cited an email one Ivy principal sent to a subordinate: "ah, Madoff, you omitted one possibility—he's a fraud!" Ivy didn't disclose its suspicions to clients, Schneiderman said, and falsely told them that "we have no reason to believe there is anything improper in the Madoff operation." Madoff's multibillion-dollar Ponzi scheme was revealed in December 2008. He is serving a 150-year prison sentence.

—Editorial

No. 4
OSPIRG to Host Forum on Hunger, Homelessness November 14, 2012

Southern Oregon University's OSPIRG chapter will host "Ashland Unroofed," a forum on hunger and homelessness in Ashland, beginning at 6 tonight in SOU's Cascade Complex, Hawthorne classroom.

Panel members will include Keith Haxton and Kristi Wright, both of Legalize Sleep, Aaron Fletcher of Homefree Hostels and Oneta Cantlon, an SOU student representative.

Among the topics the panel will discuss are proposals to provide a shelter for Ashland's homeless residents.

denigrate rather than rationally refute the others' plans? What happened to the honor of serving your country? Oh well, no matter who won, we can return to our recliners and continue to complain about what's wrong with the country (while apathy again recaptures our efforts). No problem, we can find out everything we need to know by listening to the experts (i.e., "news media"). They'll tell us the truth, right? Perhaps most of us feel that no matter what we do, nothing will change, which seems to be the case. I can't understand why any thinking person would vote for a man who did nothing but blame his predecessor for all of the problems and then had the temerity to ask for another four years.

—Murray LaHue, Phoenix

No. 5
Greed Is the Threat

I hear talk of stimulating the economy. Doesn't it stimulate the economy when consumers are forced to pay exorbitant prices for practically everything? There is no longer any relationship, however remote, between the value of the thing and its price. This is when we congratulate corporations on creating employment opportunities of minimum wage, part-time jobs with no benefits? The greatest threat to this country's integrity and stability is greed—not Afghanistan.

—Wayne Richards, Medford

No. 6
Nothing Will Change

Dr. Martin Luther King said: "free at last, free at last God Almighty, I'm free at last!" Now, after being subjected to endless campaigning (a longer period that I can remember), we are finally free of the bombast, accusations, lies, arrogance and made up "facts." What happened to the honest discourse regarding the issue and each candidates plan for solving? Why must we denigrate rather than rationally refute the others plans? What happened to the honor of serving your country? Oh well, no matter who won, we can return to our recliners and continues to complain about what's wrong with the country (while apathy again recaptures our efforts). No problem, we can find out everything we need to know by listening to the experts (i.e. "news media"). They'll tell us the truth, right? Perhaps most of us feel that no matter what we do, nothing will change, which seems to be the case. I can't understand why any thinking person would vote for a man who did nothing but blame his predecessor for all of the problems and then had the temerity to ask for another four years.

—Murray LaHue, Phoenix

No. 7
Ranks of American Poor Rise to 49.7 Million

Washington—The ranks of America's poor edged up last year to a high of 49.7 million, based on a new census measure that takes into account medical costs and work-related expenses. The numbers released Wednesday by the Census Bureau are part of a newly developed supplemental poverty measure.

—Editorial

No. 8
County Rate of Homeless

Jackson County continues to have one of the highest rates of homeless students in the state; according to figures released Wednesday the Oregon Department of Education, the Medford school district had the third highest population of homeless students—1,235—in the state, with only the larger, urban districts of Portland and Beaverton registering higher numbers. "Our numbers have been consistent we hired for the last few years," said Mary Ferrell, director of Maslow Project, a homeless youth outreach center in Medford. From 2004 to 2010, Medford had the second highest number of homeless students in the state, second only to Beaverton, a district with about three times the number of students. The number of homeless students in Medford means that 9.7 percent or nearly one in ten students, lack a fixed, regular, or adequate nighttime residence, a definition provided by the McKinney-Vento require schools across the country to count homeless students.

—Editorial

No. 9
Problems Are Serious

How serious are the problems confronting America? Consider the following:

1. Almost half of our people pay no taxes.
2. Sixty years ago, we were the richest nation on earth, now we are the greatest debtor nation.
3. We have been fighting a war in Afghanistan going on eleven years-isn't it time to get out?
4. Our government borrows 40 percent of everything they spend each month.
5. We are still giving out foreign aid with borrowed money.
6. We owe China $13 trillion and Japan almost a trillion dollars.
7. The interest on our debt is $9 billion a week or $468 billion a year.
8. Our debt surpassed 100 percent of our gross domestic product.
9. We take in from taxes $2 trillion a year, but spend over $3 trillion.

I could go on with facts such as these, but isn't it time we clean house in the Senate, Congress, and White House? We need people and government with godly principles who can follow a budget, and wouldn't it be nice if they even had a little common sense?

—Gordon De Vos, Medford, ¾/12

No. 10
Protest Encampments Bring Plight
of Homeless into Focus

One result of the Occupy by Wall Street movement is increasing awareness about the plight of homeless residents in cities all across the nation. Here in the Eugene-Springfield area, where hundreds of people have taken to the streets and parks to protest corporate greed in myriad other social and economic ills, the burning question arises: Who are the homeless?

Of course, there is no single answer and no single face of homelessness, but one thing recent events have proven yet again is that being homeless does not mean that one is necessarily dysfunctional in public. Nor does it mean that our homeless neighbors cannot contribute to a society, participate in self-governance, or get involved with community issues.

Yes, there are challenges to having people living in the public space, but these challenges posed recently occupy the Eugene were not created by homeless residents.

Organizations and entities that work to improve the lives of homeless people have long known that the majority of the resident homeless population is comprised of individuals who generally want to get along and live in peace. In these tough economic times, the growing homeless population in the Eugene-Springfield area includes those who have been living at low end of the socioeconomic strata for years. These are not people moving in from someplace else, but vulnerable neighbors who have now lost shelter.

It has been impressive how quickly the Eugene city government, the Eugene police department and other community leaders have been able to mobilize and solve problems to create safe, public space for the occupy Eugene protesters. In a matter of hours, meetings were called and decisions made—there has been compromise and creativity, and we can be proud of that. If this can be done for the temporary homeless-by-choice protesters, why can't we do this for homeless neighbors who do not have a warm shower and safe beds waiting for them?

We already have some successful models to respond to homelessness: the Egan warming centers are kicking off their fourth season, relying on hundreds of volunteers and the donations and contributions of many. A significant number of the Egan volunteers are people who are or have been homeless and who want to give back to a community that has reached out to them.

We also have a successful overnight parking program that provides dispersed, permitted, and regulated camping for homeless people throughout the city. This program, administered by St. Vincent de Paul, provides overnight parking for small, controlled numbers in parks, church parking lots, business lots, and other spaces.

The number of spaces available, however, is inadequate. Last winter, St. Vincent de Paul kept a waiting list of more than eighty people. What about all those homeless residents who don't have vehicles? The time has come to extend the camping program to include dispersed tent or canvas camping options.

We are not advocating and unregulated free-for-all, but an extension of what has worked well-both for the Occupy Eugene camping in the long-standing vehicle camping spots provided by business, churches and individuals.

There are currently forty to sixty permitted campers with vehicles in and around Eugene. Some are living on church property but many are peacefully and productively living on private lots, business properties in other locations. In fact, many businesses have found that having someone "camping" on their property deters theft and vandalism. The number of places should be increased.

In addition, allowing dispersed camping for those who are without vehicles could go a long way toward alleviating the basic challenges facing many homeless residents: having a place to stay warm and dry, legal occupation of public space instead of being at risk of breaking the law, and having a legal, safe place to go to the bathroom (Port-a-Pots are provided at each site as part of the dispersed camping program).

Legal dispersed canvas camping does not eliminate the need for Egan warming centers, but it is a cost-effective way to start to address the growing resident homeless population in and around Eugene. The

Occupy Wall Street movement has brought the plight of the homeless to the forefront of our collective consciousness. Now is the perfect time to continue the creative collaborative work of trying to lessen the impact of the current economic crisis on our most vulnerable neighbors.

Homeless people have been participating in the protests both as activists and representatives of those most battered by economic status quo. Our city officials have been stellar in their response and ability to work with the Occupy movement.

Surely we can apply the same capacity to respond by taking tangible, new steps to ease some of the challenges of homelessness.

No. 11
Lead by Example

Kudos to the retired Air Force master sergeant Sidney A. Stitt for his letter of February 7.

He inspired me to look into military bases. I found there were 737 American military bases sprawled across the globe in 2005.

Here's a quote from the Chalmers Johnson book *Nemesis: The Last Days of the American Republic*:

"With more than 2,500,000 US personnel serving across the planet and military bases spread across each continent, it's time to face up to the fact that our American democracy has spawned a global empire."

This is an obscenity, and with the vast number of citizens dying for the lack of health care, Oregon having the highest percentage of starving children in the US, plus that infrastructure that needs attention, it is time we looked at the arrogance and paranoia that puts us in the position and defines our country.

The US should lead by peaceful progress, by the demilitarizing, by taking care of our citizens with in all-inclusive healthcare system, by seeing that no one goes hungry, that our infrastructure is the best. Let us be a nation that is admired, not feared, that leads by example, not force; and that is renowned for our humanity.

—Victor Rogers, Ashland

No. 12
Occupy Washington

Occupying Oakland so nut and raisin farmers can't send out their products only hurts farmers who already have it tough to make a living. Where's "Occupy Washington," where the real perpetrators are?

Our founding fathers knew very well about greed and human nature. That's why they founded a government with checks and balances, four-year presidential terms, and laws against corruption. Our political lenders now have thrown these laws by the wayside. Clinton got rid of the Glass-Steagall Act, which held corporate corruption in check.

We need this law back! Let's investigate John Paulson, the CEO of Goldman Sachs, who persuaded Obama and Congress to bail out his company, and earned $4 billion last year. CEOs of corporations shouldn't be able to earn hundreds of millions of dollars, neither should people in Congress. Money corrupts and corruption is what's hurting America.

Our founding fathers gave us the best government in the world, and the tools to keep it that way. Somewhere along the way, our government hijacked by lobbyists, corrupt politicians, elitists, and unions. Now we need to pass laws to bring back the government to the people, while we still can!

—Richard Davenport, Medford

No. 13
Now We Get to Hate TV?

With the sale of KTVL Channel 10, another conservative media group buys into airways in the southern Oregon. All we have here now is "hate radio" 24/7 mix with a little sports and public radio. Now they are taking over local television station.

The Sinclair Group, the new owners of KTVL muffled Nightline when Ted Koppel read the names of the service people killed when we invaded Iraq. They preempted prime time run a propaganda film against John Kerry when he was running for president. They broad-casted an infomercial against Pres. Obama, claiming he was receiving campaign money from Muslim terrorist organization Hamas when he was running for president. Just what the Valley needs—more hate propaganda.

—Tom Smith, Eagle Point

No. 14
Why I Am Angry

Several years ago, I was all set for retirement. My home was worth more than the mortgages on it and there would be enough left for a down payment on a smaller property. My plan was to downsize and live happily ever after.

Then along came the greed of corporate America, the big banks and mortgage brokers. My property now is worth far less than what was owed on it, and my retirement income wouldn't cover the payments and taxes. I am now facing foreclosure and loss of my assets to cover mortgage deficiencies. I know that my situation is mirrored in millions of cases.

The government bailed out the greedy banks and mortgage companies, saying they were too big to fail. Do you believe that? Has anybody been punished for ruining so many lives? No! Do I believe in our government? All they do is take; we are in for some serious times may well destroy our way of life.

This has happened at our county level—outrageous benefits and perks to the top administrator, but do the commissioners do anything about it? Wake up, America!

—David B. Hammond, Medford

No. 15
Where Are All the Forward Thinkers?

I'm very curious to know where all the progressive thinkers are.

I used to think that Ashland was a progressive place to live, full of old-school organizers and young thinkers who see injustice in the world and would work to bring about change. I feel now that we have all become complacent in our warm little homes, cable TV, and beverages or substances that make us feel nothing. We are afraid we may lose what we have and we ignore those who have nothing. We go around spouting off about how "PC" we are because we recycle or have a "Peace Now" bumper sticker on our giant SUV in which we transport maybe two people.

Where are all the organizers and people who really care about others? Are their brains numbed to the plight of the world?

Wake up, Ashland, and reclaim our place as a truly progressive and caring city. Let's stop the gentrification of this beautiful place and show how we want true equality and not just give the lip the service that most of us use to make ourselves look good. I look forward to any response, as it means you are awake.

—Alan Lee Wattenberg, Ashland

No. 16
Why Americans Are in the Streets

Here's why Americans have taken to the streets: NAFTA outsourced millions of our family wage jobs, the 2000 presidential election was stolen, the 2001 inauguration demonstrators were herded into wire mesh "free speech" zones, huge tax cuts for the 1 percent were shoved through Congress, the Medicare drug plan turned out to be a gift to the drug companies, we were lied into two wars, fought on borrowed money and at cost of four thousand American lives, deregulated bankers caused a near depression and were bailed out with taxpayers' money. Then they gave themselves million-dollar bonuses. The savings of millions were stolen while their mortgages went under water and homes foreclosed. The earned rights of seniors (social security) and Medicare were put up for trade for more tax cuts for the 1 percent. Thirty years of GDP growth ended up in the bank accounts of the 1 percent. Congress largely became a club of new millionaires on the payrolls of lobbyists, corporations were made equal to American citizens, and our chance for a national health care system was bargained away to become a gift to the insurance companies. Are we angry? You bet. Occupy Wall Street is the first step to straighten out this mess. A long hard fight has begun.

—Bruce Barnes, 11/11/12, Ashland

No. 17
Justice for All

Our Justice Department prosecutes Wall Street insider traders but our people in Congress have made insider trading legal for themselves. That's how congressional members can enter Congress with less than a million dollars and become multimillionaires within a few years. Massey coal mine supervisors were told, "Move coal, don't fix safety violations." Twenty-nine minors died, with no prosecutions. Big banks hired people to do nothing but sign fraudulent mortgage foreclosure documents, with no prosecutions. President Bush, using more signing statements than all other presidents combined, assumed dictatorial powers, trampled our constitutional rights, violated international treaties, started two illegal wars, and ran our country into virtual bankruptcy, with no prosecution. BP violated safety rules, eleven died in a Texas refinery and caused the worst oil spill in history, with no prosecutions. While exercising our First Amendment right to peaceful assembly, demonstrators were gassed, clubbed, kicked, and pepper sprayed by police, resulting in one policeman getting what amounts to two weeks' paid vacation. Should our Pledge of Allegiance be changed to "one nation under God, indivisible, with liberty and justice for all who can afford it"?

—Sidney Stitt, 12/11/12

No. 18
Big Changes Needed

I am eighty-three years old and have a lifetime dream to see the book *Looking Backward*, by Edward Bellamy in 1888, made into a movie. It would promote Technocracy, Inc., a nonprofit organization with the scientific answers to the economic mess made by the private capitalist system owned by 3 percent of our population, who control all production and distribution to the other 97 percent of the population. Its bottom line is profit. They divert the huge excess of goods and services to making wars and preparing for wars all over the world. That huge waste of goods and services should go to raising the standard of living for every man, woman, and child in the USA. The time is long past due to create a system that is for the people, by the people, and of the people, for equal justice to all, not just for the 3 percent millionaires and billionaires who control all the politicians, both Democrats and Republicans, and the news media of all kinds. Check out the book *Looking Backward* in the library and www.technocracyinc.org. That would bring a happiness and standard of living never known before.

—E. D. Vongehr

No. 19
Occupiers Are Heroes

Bravo to the occupiers of all the cities of America and to our own. I think there are some points to be made at this time. The first is to offer our pride in the courage, intelligence, and devotion that these protestors have displayed to the world. The second point is the radical message that many of the protestors have put forth. It is not enough to reform the system. Many are calling for a structural organic shift from outmoded and dysfunctional capitalism to a new, more cooperative functional government and economic system. Thirdly, we all as Americans should be ashamed and outraged by the brutality and unconstitutional attack on unarmed people who are hardly a match to a police force in full riot gear. Police forces brutal enough in places like Oakland to send an Iraq war veteran and protestor to the hospital in Oakland in a coma. There is of course much more to say about this movement that has buoyed the spirits of us all and changed the dialogue in Main Street America. They are our heroes. We must all join then dand support them in any way we can.

—Cynthia Zavatski, 11/12

No. 20
Dump the Greedy Old Party

The system is broken, is the common label describing Washington. But it isn't the system; it is one element of that system. As Congress considers issues confronting our nation, Republican Party leaders repeatedly identify their priority as limiting President Obama to one term: they display no interest in what is best for the nation. As the president and the Democrats propose to get America back to work and solve our problems, Republicans consistently reject even those ideas that were originally Republican proposals. They used to be the Grand Old Party but are now serving only the top 1 percent and short-term corporate mega-profits, ignoring the rest of us: GOP now means "Greedy Oid Party." They reject taxing the top 1 percent at a fair rate, refuse taxing corporations escaping tax breaks for corporations making record profits. They argue the expanding gap between rich and poor is fair and reject the science of climate change because addressing the problem might reduce income for the 1 percent that funds their campaigns. The Greedy Old Party represents government of the 1 percent, by the 1 percent . . . and for the 1 percent. It is time the 99 percent tum the GOP out.

—Alan Journet, Ashland, 11/11/12

No. 22
Letter to the Editor
A Scientific Government Is Needed

In response to the letters of James Snyder 5/9/11, Dan Fellman 5/12/11: Corporations own the government and all politicians. Money rules, profit is the bottom line. The present system contradicts the basic rights of millions of unemployed, homeless, and destitute to life, liberty, and the pursuit of happiness, mainly to have a job. The present system fails in many ways. The decadent system is controlled by the power of money held by less than 5 percent of the total population. Bribery "lobbying" controls all the politicians. It is no wonder a religious group believes God is going to put an end to mankind's failure to govern itself.

If our tax system can finance billions and trillions for wars all over the world for killing and destruction, surely that machine and human energy can be directed toward the basic needs of our fellow brothers and sisters, as predicted by Edward Bellamy in his 1888 book *Looking Backward* very high standard of living for all, including the rich. No wars necessary. Prisons emptied. Huge improvement in mental and physical health. From 1930 to 1932, famous engineers, scientists, and economists researched a scientific functional way to govern. Check out technocracyinc.org, a nonprofit organization.

Edmond D. Vongehr
1432 Siskiyou Blvd.
Medford, OR 97504
Public call: 541-661-5325
Editor: Please use my phone number
Eighty-five-year-old WW2 vet
Retired, self-employed
Ins. Broker-real estate, etc.
2/11/11
Dropped off

No. 23
The Divided States of America

We are a divided nation and united we stand, divided we fall. It's the rich against the other 90 percent of Americans. The rich own and control all politicians, all news sources and thereby control the government and the private capitalist economic system.

Their bottom line is profit regardless of the consequences of harm to the other 90 percent of their fellow citizens. This so-called free enterprise system is responsible for the following:

Millions of people unemployed, homeless, hungry, begging on the streets, foreclosed. The largest jail and prison population on earth. The largest military forces and wars all over the world. All supported by lies and misinformation. That huge waste of human and machine energy that kills and destroys just to keep the system alive. That failed godless system could be changed to a scientific functional government that represents all the people on an equal basis. This system was researched from 1920 to 1932 by a group of scientists, engineers, and economists. That nonprofit organization is known as Technocracy Inc. (at www. Technocracyinc.org). The changes would create a standard of living and lifestyle never known before, a truly United States of America.

Edmond D. Vongehr
1432 Siskiyou Blvd.
Medford, OR 97504
541-661-5325

No. 24
Take the Money Out

In response to the letter from David B. Hamman on March 30, 2012, regarding our present corporate greed system and private capitalist system, and letters from Victor Rogers and retired Air Force Sgt. Sidney Stitt, regarding our 2.5 million military people all over the world. Nothing will ever change as long as our politicians control the political and economic system that has failed time after time. It is a greed system that is controlled by the power of money, and all politicians. With the millions of unemployed workers, our greed system could not stand another 2.5 million to enter the labor force. The private capitalist system no longer works. A twelve-year study from 1920 to 1932 by a group of famous engineers, scientists, and economists headed by Howard Scott put together a national plan for a scientific functional government. The plan operates without money and uses "energy certificates" to distribute all goods and services. It takes the profit motive out of the system, once and for all. Check out www.technocracyinc.org or call 360-366-1012 or call 541-661-5325, Edmond Dantes Vongehr, Medford.

No. 25
Why We Need Government

An attorney's comment on a *New York Times* article about the Costa Concordia's partial sinking in Giglio harbor, quoted here without added comment

This disaster is a perfect example of why robust government regulation of private industry is not just important but indispensable. Private industry's pursuit of ever greater profit always, always, always tempts it to cut comers and private industry will yield to that temptation in the absence of strong government oversight. There are endless examples, such as the recent toxic mortgage disaster that blew up the world's economy. Yes, there can be too much government, but there can also be too little, often resulting, as in this case, in the avoidable deaths of human beings and a potential environmental disaster. Ever since Ronald Reagan's presidency, the right-wing mantra has been: government is the problem, not the solution. I hope my right-wing friends will abandon such simpleminded sloganeering and realize that what is needed is a sensible government/industry relationship that works to safeguard good capitalism and simultaneously to undo and avoid the descent into toxic capitalism. For capitalism without government oversight is like a pro football game without referees, and the result will always be brutal and cruel.

—Hartley Anderson, 5/12, Medford

No. 26
Where Is Compassion?

I am a single father raising two teenagers. I am appalled and disgusted by the current state of politics and the blatant hatred and greed and avarice that I see coming from many groups in our nation. While I am disgusted by the behaviors exhibited by Republicans and Democrats, I am even more concerned by the failure of the church to stand up for the poor and oppressed. Instead, the church has been poisoned by the unholy alliance with the Republican Party. While the Republicans are trying to cut taxes for the wealthy and corporate elite, they are suggesting that the poor and middle class shoulder the burden of a heavy deficit by cutting vital social programs. Instead of speaking out and standing in the gap for the poor and oppressed, the church has been silent and complicit. However, the Bible is clear that Jesus was an advocate for the poor and oppressed. Where is the compassion that Americans are so proud of! In my humble opinion, the church leaders need to rethink their political alliances and simply follow the scripture "Love thy neighbor." Helping the wealthy is not a priority in the New Testament. Compassion for your fellow man is.

—Ralph Bagley, Medford, 5/11

No. 27
Ike Would Weep

Thoughts on a Veterans Day following a presidential election: conservative Republicans tend not so much to like veterans as much as they like systems, weaponry, and munitions, and the contracts that go to major systems, weaponry, and munitions contractors, companies, and contributors. By spending as much as possible on "defense" projects, conservative Republicans can say: We are sorry we cannot support this very important social project. The budget just won't allow it. See also: aircraft carriers and seven of the eight budgets the Bush/ Cheney administration sent to Congress underfunding the VA. The Romney/Ryan budget would have cut VA funding over 13 percent while increasing that of the Department of Defense. The VA is not a part of the Department of Defense. Ike would weep.

—Harry Freiberg (US Navy 1967 to 1971,
Vietnam 1967 to 1968), Brookings

No. 28
Tax Cuts Do Not Equal Growth

The nonpartisan Congressional Research Office recently released a report, "Taxes and the Economy: An Economic Analysis of the Top Tax Rates Since 1945," which shows no relationship between upper income tax rates and economic growth. Two previous CRS reports,

"Shall Business and the Expiration of the 2001 Tax Rate Reductions" and "Economic Effects of Capital Gains Taxation," also support this position. Yet Speaker John Boehner and most Republican representatives continue to claim that raising taxes on the wealthy will cost jobs. Republicans continue to make these statements as dogma even though they have no basis in fact. It reminds one of their denial of manmade global warming, the consequences of which are increasingly washing up on our shores. Most of us do not even have to read CRS reports when we remember that the Bush tax cuts led to huge deficits and the biggest recession since the 1930s. We cannot find our way out of the fiscal and jobs crisis when our representatives put their own and their friends' wealth before the business of the nation. Please join me in telling our newly reelected Rep. Greg Walden to get real and stop blocking the president's tax proposals.

—Mark Heritage, Rogue River, Nov. 16, 2012

No. 29
Corporations and Profit

Understanding large corporations is not complicated.

Profit matters, everything else comes in last. This single-minded pursuit of profit, left uncensored, invariably leads to environmental plunder and pollution, dangerous working conditions, tricky advertising, unsafe products, economic upheavals, etc. Expecting corporations to voluntarily place the public good above profits is akin to hoping wolves will only prey on deer that have no youngsters to raise. Only one power prevents corporate practices from transforming society into a wasteland-government regulation. Unfortunately, government has its own dark side: power-hungry politicians, bloated budgets, wasteful spending, spoiled and arrogant government employees, political campaigns financed largely by corporations seeking to weaken regulations that diminish their profit margins. Not surprisingly, about half our crisis-weary voters despise the corporate world, while the rest consider government and its pesky regulations a blight on society. Over time, it's a workable if messy balance. Except lately, business-worshiping politicians and talking heads are preaching that the only solution to the economic disaster created by poorly regulated Wall Streeters is to peel back even more hard-won regulations and allow an unleashed capitalism to shower us with universal prosperity. You betcha. And maybe those wolves can be persuaded to leave Bambi and his mama in peace.

—Frank Long, Central Point, 10/18/11

No. 30
Now Is the Time

Leonard Pitts' October 19 column noted the protestors against Wall Street have not offered any alternative solutions to the economic and political failures they are protesting against; if only they could become aware of the twelve-year study from 1920 to 1932 by famous engineers, scientists, and economists that found the solutions and answers to our presently failed political and economic systems. The Constitution and Bill of Rights for citizens could be made truly effective, and the power of money by the I percent would no longer rule. A new system would replace the use of money. Technocracy Inc. at www.technocracyinc. Org is a nonprofit, nonpolitical educational organization. It has a technological social design for the North American continent, put together after long study. Edward Bellamy in his famous 1888 book *Looking Backward*, predicted social and economic changes such as technocracy envisions. All politicians represent themselves and the 3 percent of the money holders. The politicians would join the labor force with productive work. The change would not be socialism or communism or any other ism. It would create a society of one for all and all for one, a wonderful life for all, including the very rich.

—Edmond Dantes Vongehr, Medford, October 2011

No. 31
Journal View Is Different

The Wall Street Journal certainly has a different future in mind for the USA than I do. Calling Medicare "the main driver of the fiscal crisis" (editorial reprinted in the *Mail Tribune*, December 28, 2012) is offensive and dangerous. What about not taxing the wealthiest 1 percent? What about spending billions—or is it trillions?—of dollars on the corporations that profit from our endless military adventures? My parents, who lived through the Great Depression to burst with American pride as they helped win World War Two, believed that America's greatest contribution was providing opportunity for ordinary working people. The keystones were public education for the young and some security in old age, not milking the masses to create, enormous fortunes for a tiny elite. The Journal decries the 3 percent above GDP growth rate of Medicare costs. Did it also editorialize against Bank of America's proposal to protect the 400 percent profit margin on debit card purchases? Guess it depends on your perception of who is a citizen of this country, the people who live, work, and die here or the corporations.

—Marie Reeder, Rogue River, January 2012

No. 32
Fix Gas Prices Now

I would like to ask our president and the legislators of our country a question about economic recovery if gas prices rise to $5.00 a gallon or more. What do they think is going to happen if people have even less money to spend on essentials such as food, clothing, medical expenses, much less other products and services? Well, it would appear there will be no recovery for now and in the distant future. Maybe I am way off here, so I would like them to tell me to the best of their "ability" what they think will be the outcome of another oil company ransom. They are the ones who are supposed to have our best interests in mind, right? We elected them and pay them to do what's right for the people in this country first. It appears they are more interested in being elected and telling us that they can turn things around than really helping anyone. They have done very little in the past, so I do not expect anything better for our future. Oh nuts, I forgot one thing: I helped put some of them in office. I guess this is partly my fault.

—Jim Surowski, Rogue River, March 2012

No. 33
We Cannot Have Both

Republicans intend to kill President Obama's jobs bill mostly because they are against whatever he is for, but also because it included a modest increase in taxes for the rich. Taxes are the lowest they have been in generations, and the national debt has never been higher. Neither the Republican nor the Democratic budget proposals even eliminate the deficit, much less reduce the debt. It could not be more obvious that we need to both cut spending and raise more revenue. Raising it from those who can most afford it is just common sense. Republicans call it class warfare. In reality, class warfare includes such GOP pastimes as denying the poor access to health care and sabotaging the Wall Street financial reforms. But Republicans' contempt for reality is well known. Obama's birth, death panels, the global warming hoax, why bother with facts when you can make up your own? Wake up, America. In the US, 1 percent of the population owns 40 percent of the wealth, while 15 percent live in poverty . . . that's class warfare.

—Michael Steely, October 2011, Medford

No. 34
Time to Create Jobs

The recent news conference by President Obama put into focus where we are now nationally on the big issue of jobs and what the two major parties have to offer. The president, after he and congressional Democrats have worked hard to avert three shutdowns over the debt ceiling and the budget, has challenged the country and the Republicans in particular, to get something done about creating jobs. Public pressure on elected officials is crucial. The Republicans-led House has really done nothing to pass legislation to create jobs and since they took over, the economic situation has worsened, their agenda of cuts and rollbacks of regulations is counterproductive. And keep in mind Republican senators are holding up confirmation of a well-qualified person to fill the role of consumer watchdog, under the Frank-Dodd legislation. The reason: they like the candidate but do not like the law that passed, but so what? Barack Obama may not be Secretariat but he is the best horse I intend to ride because he is running in the right direction now and the other horses in the race are on a different track than I am on. Maybe the Occupy energy will wake up the beast. It's time.

—Steve Haskell, Ashland, 10/13/11

No. 35
Letter Was Right On

In response to Victor Rogers' letter on June 7 about foreign military bases and sustainability, all I can say is right on. I've thought the same things about America's huge military presence all over the world, and about how that incredible expenditure of energy could be better used. It is not a matter of American security. In my opinion, the threats to our nation are best dealt with via intelligence / police / Special Forces action rather than full military response, invasions, and occupations. If we keep swatting flies with cruise missiles, we would be more effective in the fight against terrorism and more secure at home. Mr. Roger's point about the enmity that American forward bases cause worldwide is a very valid one. Just think of the resources Americans would have at their disposal if we got out of the empire/nation-building business and focused on rebuilding our own country. We could balance the budget and have music education in middle schools.

—Michael Whipple, Medford, June 2011

No. 36
Seeking Intelligence

If there is any intelligence around, I request some exposure to it. Is that expecting too much? Most if not all, the letters to the editor seem to be written by people who pretend to be smart but who in reality only people who have been taught what to think by themselves or some other median (say TV). If anyone doubts this to be true, I suggest thinking (although this may be a first for brainwashed people). This is not an attempt to be "elitist" or some other derogatory title, it is simply a statement of fact. We are in the throes of an awful depression that easily equates to that of the 1930s, and yet there is no admission to that in the mainstream press, which is you. Your articles keep yapping about a recovering recession, and the facts are obvious at the markets, stores, gas pumps, etc. that this is not even the middle of this devastating depression. Have you scanned the real estate business lately? Are you willing, as a "public service body," to expose these truths? Or like the US government's typical denial, do you wish to simply continue this farce?

—Duane Sample, Jacksonville, Feb. 2011

No. 37
Basic Economics Missing

I am a retailer. When I opened my first retail store in 1965, 100 percent of the merchandise was made in the US. When I closed my last business last year, 99 percent was made overseas. I counted only six items made in the US. What I observed over the years is that few people understand basic economics. It simply not taught in the school system through college. Back in the end of the 1970s, the Washington establishment, both Democrats and Republicans, decided that we should become a free-trade country. The flaw here is that we did not have a fair-trade policy. As a result our manufacturing proceeded to go overseas as we could not compete with the vast salary differences. The service economy does not produce wealth. Service jobs are at the low end of the salary scale. Manufacturing results in an additional six to twelve employees in the community to support each high-paid manufacturing job. The reverse happens, unemployment increases when you send jobs overseas. Think about it

—Fred A. Zerull Jr., Jacksonville, 8/9/11

No. 38
Eliminate the Root of All Evil

Money as a medium of exchange no longer works in today's society. We live in a scientific, technological, machine-producing world. Machines have replaced the need for manpower and are a cause for all the problems, beginning with unemployment of the masses.

A new means of functional government is needed to direct the huge production capacity of machinery and technology and solve most of the world's problems, including the need for wars all over the globe.

The power of money, with its control of all politicians and all news sources, prevents real changes from being made.

Famous engineers, scientists, economists, and educators in 1922 to 1932, known as the Technical Alliance, now known as Technocracy Inc., found the answers to our nonfunctional government and failed capitalist system. In 1888, Edward Bellamy wrote a famous novel that predicted a world without unemployment and all the woes created by the nonfunctional, nonscientific government of the time. A movie needs to be made of *Looking Backward* to educate everyone to possibilities of a world envisioned by Technocracy Inc.'s functional government. Everyone is welcome to check out www. technocracyinc.org except paid politicians. Continental headquarters are in Ferndale, Washington. Director in chief nationwide is George Wright, fax 360-966-2449.

—Edmond Dantes Vongehr, Medford, August 2010

No. 39
Social Justice Is Justice

Social justice is not tyranny, nor is it a code word for communism; far from these, social justice describes a system where all individuals (as far as humanly possible) not only get a fair start in life-education, security, and necessities of life-but also where the honest needs of individuals are safeguarded throughout life. Social justice is not communism; communism was a response to extreme social injustice, but as history has shown, it does not work, in part because the leadership was corrupted. Under a socially just system, individuals would benefit from their own talents and honest effort. Under the same systems though, individuals who have done well would return some of their good fortune to the system that has allowed them to prosper in the first place. Creating a more socially just system is less about politics and more about a change in values and attitude. It's a spiritual thing. It is valuing people, human well-being, dignity, and expression more than we value possessions, fame, or power. It is not an easy task to make it work; we must express our values in how we live as well as in how we vote.

—Bill McWhorter, Medford

No. 40
Confusion Won't Go Away

One of the few things the Tea Party and Occupy protestors have in common is frustration with Wall Street. Likewise, many Americans in the middle of the political spectrum express similar sentiments. Why won't this issue go away? The reason many are confused about Wall Street is because the 2008 economic crash resulted in a bank bailout that cost taxpayers billions. Even though some of the bailouts had been paid back, a palpable distrust on financial institutions remains. Since bailing out large businesses goes against a core tenet of market economics, frustration with Wall Street resonates. The deregulation of banks in 1999 and 2000 created an intense period for our nation's financial institutions. During this time, many of our commercial banks became involved in the risky derivative investments that investment banks use. When these investments created a bubble leading to the 2008 crash, wealthy financiers pleaded for assistance from the government to both stay afloat and, as it turns out, continue handing out million-dollar bonuses. As a result of the bailout, many Americans are bewildered. Ironically, many sense that free-market deregulation inadvertently led to socialism for the rich on Wall Street. This confusion just won't go away.

—Perry Casilio, Talent, 11/2/11

No. 41
GOP Tried to Ax Social Security

Many have apparently forgotten that the previous Republican administration wished to eliminate social security. They suggested people invest in the stock market instead. That would be better, they insisted, for hardworking people to invest in the stock market instead, as if we are all stock experts. The rather uncanny idea found few supporters at the time. In fact, it finds clarity only in retrospect, seeing as how shortly later, the stock market tumbled, that is to say: they knew Wall Street was going to be in very serious trouble soon. And they were all too willing to risk the American people's retirement security. Just think how awful it could have been for so many, to lose not only their retirement and investment savings but also their social security as well. I think that was rather un-American of the Republican administration.

—Patti Morey, Ashland, November 2011

No. 42
Gravely Concerned

For the first time in my eighty-two years of existence, I'm gravely concerned for the future of our country. We have had many threats in those eighty-two years from outside the country, and some from within, but I have never feared that our country would not pull together and meet the threat. This time the threat comes from within the country, and the threat is the Congress of the United States. The country is in economic chaos. People are losing homes, businesses are failing, and hundreds of thousands (millions) are out of work with little or no hope for change. This is because too many of our elected representatives have personal agendas they follow, are controlled by special interests or by greed. They have forgotten they were elected to conduct the business for all the people of the country. They have also forgotten their oath of office they swore to uphold. Several years ago, a Russian prime minister stated that the United States would never fall to an outside threat but would be taken down by forces from within the country. I cannot but fear the prophecy is about to come true.

—Paul R. Avery, Medford, 9/12

No. 43
A Few of Their Favorite Things

Things Republicans like to do:

> Present either/or arguments about complicated issue.
> Blame, criticize, and refuse to work with Democrats.
> Fear-mongering.
> Purport to be for the little guy while promoting policies that benefit the rich.
> Blend church and state.
> Keep money in politics.
> Hurry to say racism is over while doing little to make it so.
> Support prison, vengeance, and punishment over rehabilitation and justice.
> Support the notion of working hard while lowering capital gains taxes.
> Condemn health care reform without a plan to address the problem.
> Promote capitalism without constraints.
> Convince you that it is a level playing field in this country.
> Perpetuate subsidies for defense, big agriculture, and oil while cutting benefits for regular people.
> Spin issues and facts with characterizations such as "death tax" entitlements and death panels.

Both parties do many of the things mentioned above. It's just that the Republicans do it much more.

—Doug Huston, Ashland, 9/4/12

No. 44
Eyes Are Wide Open

The signs say "Wake up, America." Well, my wide-open eyes are seeing plenty. They see Republican presidential candidate courting the 1 percent at his fifty-thousand-dollar dinner. I see the 99 percent won't get crumbs, let alone cake. I see Republicans pretending our huge deficit has nothing to do with their president taking us to war in Iraq without raising taxes; no other American president has been so fiscally irresponsible. I saw them using their majority in Congress to block banking controls under the same president, yet giving huge bailouts to banks in 2008. I see them stubbornly resist necessary yet commonsense regulation, we see the same party attack a health care program that offers relief to the 99 percent, and also lowers medical costs. We watch as they ignore the two biggest threats to our continued existence: overpopulation and the resulting degradation of our environment. Wake up, 99 percent.

—Kathleen Heritage, Rogue River, 7/2012

No. 45
Tax Code Grew This Country

Regarding John Horbecks's letter: Progressive tax is not a "commie plot" nor is it a redistribution of wealth scheme designed to reward slackers. Progressive tax is what made the middle class strong, and grew the USA into the economic powerhouse that it used to be. That's right, all through the Cold War era we had a "commie" tax code (and no one noticed). It's astonishing how effective the Republicans have been at selling the horribly wrong myth that if we just give more wealth to the upper class and corporations, they will lavish us with jobs and wage increases. This ridiculous idea has been tried over and over and it has never worked; the slide started with Reagan, and we are now seeing the long-term effects. The truth is that companies hire only as many employees as they need to support the demand for their goods and services. To make matters worse, the Bush tax cuts were the principal cause of our current record debt. Next time you see a

"Wake up, America" sign, remember that what the poor uninformed owner of the sign wants is his commie tax code back.

—Keith Shirley, Medford, June 2011

No. 46
Corporations Own Government

America is unique in its government policies. Why do we have nine-year wars that cost $2 billion a week yet never lead to victory, or anything even resembling victory? Unbelievable. A superpower military somehow unable to attain victory in nine years, even against puny, low budget opponents like the Taliban. Here is why: back in 1890, America had only a handful of corporate multimillionaires—Rockefeller, Morgan, Mellon, Carnegie, etc. They correctly assumed that by infiltrating themselves and their cronies into the government, they would soon own it. Bribery was renamed "lobbying" (a completely legal activity), which made their job much easier. Freedom, liberty, and democracy were dead by 1965, existing today as pretty-sounding words, usually accompanied by flag waving, and talk about God, to rally the yokels and yahoos at voting time. Cheney's Halliburton Corp. became a handy pipeline for billions in taxpayer dollars because he had great White House connections and an obedient puppet from Crawford, Texas, doing his bidding. Soon, Halliburton was the seventh biggest corporation in the world. And people like George Will tell us (with a straight) that lobbying is harmless and should be protected as a form of free speech. Amazing . . .

—James Snyder, Medford, May 2011

No. 47
Support Taxation Fairness

With regard to Matt Witt's guest opinion, "Wall Street has us fighting over the leftovers," here's something readers can do to protest the cuts in education and basic services brought about by big corporations and billionaires not paying their fair share of taxes. At noon Tuesday, June 7, residents of Jackson County will gather at Vogel Plaza in Medford to highlight the huge tax breaks Pres. Bush gave the richest 2 percent of Americans ten years ago. Bush's tax giveaways continued a thirty-year trend of transferring wealth from the middle-class Americans to the rich. Income inequality is now at its highest peak since 1928. Oregonians can let senators Ron Wyden and Jeff Merkley, and Rep. Greg Walden know that you support HR 1224, the Fairness in Taxation Act introduced by Rep. Jan Schakowsky of Illinois that would create new tax brackets for millionaires and working Americans to help middle-class families cope with the recession. The cuts in services we are facing here in the Rogue Valley did not just happen like the weather. The Bush giveaway to millionaires is one major cause. It's time that those most able to pay start contributing their share like the rest of us.

—Caren Caldwell, Ashland, May 2011

No. 48
Democracy Is a Thing of the Past

The Supreme Court ruling that allowed corporations to spend unlimited amounts of money to elect the candidate that they can control makes democracy a thing of the past. Even foreign governments could play a deciding role. The ordinary voter has almost no options. You can support the effort to amend the Constitution or you can ignore the media ads that corporations are putting out. It doesn't seem possible that judges who had any judgment could possibly declare that corporations are the same as people.

—Norma Anderson, Ashland, July 2011

No. 49
Job Creation is the answer

Your listing of over three hundred foreclosures gives perspective to your upbeat front-page story of one fortunate mortgagee. The American economy is in a perilous and worsening condition. Only a massive infusion by means of a federal job-creating program, along with a moratorium on home foreclosures, will bring us out of the mess created by the Bush tax cuts, our irrational wars and Wall Street's fraud.

—Gerald Cavanaugh, Ashland, June 2011

No. 50
GOP Plan Is Class Warfare

The Reagan-Bush tax cuts for the wealthy were justified on the grounds that, when invested, they would have a trickle-down effect benefitting middle-and lower-income Americans. Instead, they had the opposite effect, as income was transferred from the rest of the population to the few already wealthy Americans. The most affluent 10 percent received 91 percent of the income gain and the top 1 percent received a stunning 59 percent. Historically, corporations created jobs by reinvesting profits in company growth. However, they now promote trickle-up economics by allocating corporate profits instead to maximizing shareholder profit. While downsizing companies, executives rewarded themselves with stocks and then even purchased stocks to bolster shareholder and their own incomes. A tax system levying a smaller percentage on stock dividends than regular salary further encouraged this transition. The Ryan budget plan continues Republican trickle-up economics. Ryan proposes to reduce the budget by $4.3 trillion over ten years by cutting programs that benefit most Americans. Simultaneously, he would replace these savings by continuing $4.3 trillion in tax breaks to the already wealthy. Republicans again want to redirect tax dollars from the majority of Americans to the already wealthy. This is class warfare! And still corporations paying zero taxes are untouched.

—Alan Journet, Ashland, June 2011

No. 51
See in Shades of Gray

I read in the Friday, December 23 paper a letter from a gentleman who in response to the Occupy movement echoed some key thoughts of Ayn Rand, author of the conservative tome Atlas

Shrugged, namely, that self-interest is the key motivating force of capitalism, not self-sacrifice. In my youth, I was a devotee of Atlas Shrugged. It reduced people to simple terms: producers and moochers. But later, I learned that life is not so black and white, with self-interested capitalism on one side and wealth-confiscating socialism on the other. Life is a thing where good men are laid off for no good reason, where good families sleep in their cars in December. Self-interest devoid of concern for our fellow man . . . well, it may have sounded good on paper when I was a kid. It may have made the world seem a simpler place to a young person about to set sail, but Dickens showed us a stark world of black and white through the eyes of a fellow who had a dream and woke a changed man. May 2012 be the year we all learn to see in shades of gray, God bless us, everyone.

—Leslie Morgan, Medford, 12/11

No. 52
Letter Was Right On

James Snyder succinctly and eloquently hit the nail on the head in his letter of Monday, May 9, "Corporations Own Government." Meanwhile, Ron Smith suggests that Obama has taken credit for an operation that was initiated by the Bush administration. Sorry, Ron, not possible: George W. Bush in office seven and a half years after 9/11, no Osama bin Laden. Barack Obama in office eighteen months . . . bingo. Why? Because the Bush administration needed Osama bin Laden to keep us afraid and not ask questions while the Halliburton Corp. and the rest of the "defense" industry looted the National Treasury to the tune of $2 billion a week for years and years while the rest of us quibble over spending peanuts to educate our young or care for our elders. It is not possible that George Will is so dense as to believe what he writes. He is a willing instrument of the corporate machinery that exists to separate the American people from our money. The saddest victims among us are the patriots who consistently vote against their own interests, and send their children to fight the wars.

—Dan Fellman, Ashland, 5/11/11

No. 53
Prosperity Requires Balance

The economy of the past few decades has been characterized by a growing imbalance between the investor class (mainly rich) and the consumer class (mainly the middle class). The first accumulated so much money that a lot of irresponsible loans and speculative investments were made, which set things up for a bust. The middle class, squeezed by the artificially high cost of housing and seeing many of its good jobs shipped overseas became so loaded with debt that its ability to consume became stalled. We now live with the consequences. Republicans believe that more money in the hands of investors will create jobs, but does this make any sense? To do business, you must have buyers, so private business investment will be ineffective until there is a consumer class that is once again able to buy products. The counterproductive imbalance between the investor class and the consumer class is inherent to our problems and will only get worse under Republican programs favoring the rich. The essential corrective is to raise taxes on the rich and use the money for public works projects that would directly strengthen the consumer class, restoring a more productive balance between the classes.

—Nicholas Follansbee, Medford, 9/11/12

No. 54
Republicans Can't Say Yes

After another GOP walkout, President Obama asked rhetorically, "Can they say yes to anything?" Not to him. Their policy of being against whatever he's for has hampered and delayed our economic recovery. Now they don't even want to pay our bills because Obama says we should. Republicans would rather plunge us into economic chaos than do anything he wants, no matter how necessary. Obama's mistake has been treating them like grown-ups. He should have told them he wanted to default on our loans. Then they wouldn't have been able to raise the debt ceiling fast enough.

—Michael Steely, Medford, 7/11/11

No. 55
What Are We Doing?

While watching television, I saw a small clip with Rachel Maddow. She commented on how the past generations of this great land had built infrastructure such as our national highway system and Hoover Dam. She then asked, "What are we doing?" The only answer I could give went like this: we are letting our infrastructure crumble; we are destroying our public education system that, for decades, produced many of the brilliant minds we have today. We are protecting the banking industry that brought us the depression we find ourselves in today; we are abandoning our seniors and the very young through draconian cuts to much-needed programs. We have spent well over $4 trillion, and still counting, on two unnecessary wars. We have a party that, in my opinion, would rather take this country down into the financial abyss than give our first black president any kind of political victory. I hope things will change for the better, but I won't hold my breath.

—Lindsay Paulk, White City, 7/11/11

No. 56
What Republicans Want

Republicans care for little more than wealth and power. Our country is in dire straits right now. We were put here by the Bush administration and its friends on Wall Street and with help from the Supreme Court. They will never be satisfied until they control the entire government and are spending unlimited amounts of money to convince the American electorate that it's the fault of Democrats and the black "he's half white" president. To that end, they are doing everything they can to destroy recovery and job growth. Wake up, America! What are Republicans good for? Like war, absolutely nothing.

—Jack Eagleson, Medford, 8/11/1 I

No. 57
This Isn't America

Every time I try to save, something happens—the water line, the lawn mower, my truck, it's constant. I can only go to the grocery store a few times a week because I can't afford the gas. I conserve water by not flushing every time I pee. I use dollar-store flashlight batteries to hold down the electric bill. In the winter, I bundle up to keep the heat bills down. Doubters are welcome to come and see. Social security is no longer to increase benefits for those who need. The money, your money, is being held in reserve for "private enterprise" for the future. The elderly are being punished for not being well-to-do, yet we worked hard for so long, and for so little. The only trickle down these people get are the tears on their faces. No matter what you have now, when social security goes, so do you. Next in line is the upper middle class. This isn't America. It isn't even a democracy any longer. This is a capitalistic state of greed, power, and self-interest. It's staggering, almost as if Cheney was still the puppet master of the Republican Party.

—Frank Mequish, Medford, 8/1/11

No. 58
Grant Them Serenity

When we elected President Obama, Republicans showed their contempt by vowing to make him fail. Their strategy was simple: stonewall and filibuster, deliberately delaying our recovery from the recession, and then blame it on him. Meanwhile, fringe elements took to the streets, raving hysterically about Obama being a foreign-born commie/Nazi/socialist. Republicans liked their style and sought their support. Be careful what you wish for, the lunatics have taken over the asylum. So now they have candidates for highest office bragging about how much they love Jesus but hate giving health care to the poor, denouncing science as a hoax and promising to lighten the tax burden on the rich. Anyone tainted by reason is labeled a wacko in name only, or wino. The party is currently being driven by rage and resentment almost as by corporate greed. Rush Limbaugh's bloated belligerence is the new face of the GOP. Some people apparently find it entertaining, but is that whose finger you want on the nuclear trigger? For years they've been wallowing in spite, to the nation's detriment. When President Obama is reelected, may God grant them the serenity to get over it.

—Michael Steely, Medford, 11/20/11

No. 59
Go After Bigger Fish

Judging by the prosecution's outrage in a recent US District Court case charging conspiracy to defraud the government, you might think the federal government's finally cracking down on the miscreants that demolished our economy. The defendants hatched an elaborate fraud designed to game the system, lining (their) pockets at the taxpayers' expense. Bank scam? Mortgage con? Not quite. Two Grants Pass sisters and their mom lied on application forms when one daughter obtained assistance to rent a family-owned house. They pleaded guilty, must repay nearly $13,000, and perform thirty days community service. The feds also sought thirty days in jail. I don't know these people or condone their acts; they should pay. But going after jail time seems heavy handed when despite massive evidence of serious criminality, hardly a single major player in the banking, mortgage, or brokerage industries who gamed the system for billions has even been charged-let alone imprisoned. If you have an army of lawyers and PR flacks, and own influential allies.

(Think revolving door between Wall Street and government.) You are too big to fail and too powerful to prosecute. And the whole greedy scheme, far from fixed, is primed to melt down again.

—Rand Hill, Grants Pass, 11/12

No. 60
Depression Is Here Again

1. Millions of people out of jobs, homeless, or in prison, all money-related crimes, with begging on the streets across America
2. The highest prison population of all advanced nations
3. Daily reports of corruption in both public services and private industry, city, state, and national, mostly money based crimes-it is immoral and appalling.
4. The present system is truly unfair, unjust, immoral and a disgrace to the intelligence of the American people.

More than eighty years ago, a group of famous scientists, engineers, and educators undertook a twelve-year study of the North American social and economic systems. In those twelve years of study, they put together a scientific plan that would replace the existing "private" capitalist system that has failed time after time since the Industrial Revolution. Only 5 percent or less of the population own or control, with the power of their money, all politicians, courts, and news agencies, and distortion and lies keep the public misinformed and uninformed. For the real truth, check out www technocracyinc. org, national headquarters in Ferndale, Washington.

—Edmond D. Vongehr, Medford, 7/20/10

No. 61
I'm Delighted Obama Won

I am a seventy-four-year-old white man who was an engineer at Boeing and McDonnell Douglas. And I am delighted that Barack Obama's values for America have beaten back those of Republicans, who believe high-income whites should run this country, primarily for their own benefit. Greediness and racial discrimination are death knells of a country.

—Hartley Anderson, Medford, 11/8/12

No. 62
A Rational Response

Bravo to the *Los Angeles Times* for taking a stand on the side of reason, logic, and the evidence (Other Views, Monday, November 5, 2012). Only the willfully blind and/or willfully destructive will describe our existing, worsening global climate catastrophe and our increasingly severe and numerous meteorological events as either acts of God or simply a passing phase. Of course, a rational response to the catastrophe will entail a transcendence of our present economic system, which is why our corporate lords and masters prefer catastrophe to any meaningful cure. Thank you, *Mail Tribune*, for raising the issue.

—Gerald Cavanaugh, Ashland, 11/9/12

No. 63
Taxes Can Create Jobs

I think the reason so many people sacrifice their interests to support conservative policies is that they assume their suffrage will shift resources toward helping our country. I know I love my country too, and I certainly would pay higher taxes or support a disproportionate military or forgo nationalized health care or quality public education or better wages if it were proven to help advance our country as a whole. The problem is that supporting those policies is what is destroying the middle class and the middle class is the core of what makes our country great. One example lowering taxes that put more money in the pockets of people that will spend it creates demand. Employers only hire as many employees as demand for their goods or services requires. You get taxed on your profits, not your operating costs, so if you reinvest profits back into a business your taxes go down. In effect, higher tax rates for the wealthy actually create more jobs. Characterizing the repeal of the Bush tax cuts as "taxing job providers" is an idiotic slogan that makes no sense whatsoever. And do we need 50,000 troops in Germany today?

—Keith Shirley, Medford, 8/16/11

No. 64
Who Created the Jobs?

Charles Olsen wrote that the only thing that ended the Great Depression was World War Two. Even though I disagree with his premise, let's look at the facts, those pesky little facts. Who created and paid for the soldiers, marines, pilots, WAVES, and WACs? The US government. Who paid for the fighter planes, bombers, gliders, destroyers, submarines, aircraft carriers and battleships? The US government. Who trained and paid for those same fighting men and the code breakers, the Seabees, the bombsights, the guns, the tanks, the ammunition, the bombs, the C rations, and email. The US government. And who paid for the doctors and nurses who tended the wounded warriors? The US government. And when the war was won, who saved Berlin? The US government's Berlin airlift. And who when it was over, created the great American middle class? The US government's GI Bill, and low-cost home loans. Ah yes, thank you, Mr. Olsen, for reminding us how our government messing around with our capitalist system and spending our hard-earned money by taxing us, saved the world.

—Mary Morsell, Medford, 8/16/11

No. 65
How Do You Change a Hopeless Situation?

We have people without jobs, begging on the streets. Our country has the largest prison and jail population of all nations.

The corruption, both in private industry and public service, is appalling. Since the Industrial Revolution, machines produce over 90 percent of all goods and services. The private capitalist is owned and controlled by less than 5 percent of the nation's wealthiest citizens. The corporations have no love or regard for their fellow brothers and sisters.

Edward Bellamy predicted in 1888, that the time would come when the industry and commerce of the country, ceasing to be conducted by a set of irresponsible corporations and syndicates of private persons at their caprice and for their profit, were finally entrusted to a single syndicate representing all the people, to be conducted in the common interest, for the common profit of the nation. That is to say, organized as one great corporation, in which all other corporations were absorbed. It became the only capitalist in place of all other capitalists. The sole employer, the final monopoly in which all previous and lesser monopolies were swallowed up. A monopoly, in the profits and economies of which all citizens shared. The epoch of trusts had ended in the great trust. In a word, the people of the United States concluded to assume the conduct of their own business, just as one hundred-odd years before they had assumed the conduct of their own government. Organizing now for industrial purposes on precisely the same grounds that they had organized for political purposes. At last, strangely late in the world's history, the obvious fact was perceived that no business is so essentially the public business as the industry and commerce on which the people's livelihood depends. And that to entrust it to private persons to be managed for private profit is a folly similar in kind, though vastly greater in magnitude, to that of surrendering the functions of political government to kings and nobles to be conducted for their personal glorification. Read Edward Bellamy's *Looking Backward*, in 1888.

—Edmond Dantes Vongehr, Medford

No. 66
What's Wrong with Our Country?

It is no wonder that the American people don't trust the government and all politicians. All politicians are controlled by money and self-interest. They will never pass laws to change the status quo. If only the huge waste of energy, both in human power and machine power, was directed to raising the standard of living of every citizen, there would be no need for wars of destruction all over the world. That huge divergement of energy and manpower toward wars and the preparation for wars all over the world. The private enterprise system and all politicians are controlled by corporations who represent less than 5 percent of the population and the long-time, so-called free enterprise system or "private enterprise." That system has failed time and time again and is a greed system with the bottom line, profit for the few and to hell with the rest of the population. Jobs are sent overseas by our kindhearted brothers. Wars and huge military forces divert huge amounts of energy, both human and machine. If these millions of military and displaced workers returned to the stagnant system of unemployed and underemployed, there would be chaos in the streets. The present system cannot be fixed when all the politicians are ruled and controlled by the money powers. We need a scientific government and judicial system that governs for all the people as predicted by Edward Bellamy in his 1888 novel *Looking Backward*.

President Obama means well, but the money powers controlling all politicians and the so-called free press he is up against insurmountable odds. The government, with taxpayers' money, has bailed out the bankrupt automobile and private banking systems. Public individuals that fail are taken over by their creditors. In this case, the American public should take over and appoint a new scientific government that is not interested in wars or the profit motive. A high standard of living for every man, woman, and child would be the motive and do away with the immoral, decadent, unfair, and truly unconstitutional system we are forced to live under since the Industrial Revolution and machine age.

—Edmond Dantes Vongehr, Medford, Oregon

No. 67
Ridiculous Communist Charge

The idea in the May 5 letter "Stop Wicked Agenda" that the majority of the elected Democrats in the House are members of the Communist Party is ridiculous. This idea belongs in the same manure bin as the ideas that any ethnic group or major religion is plotting to take over the United States. Where our real danger lies is in the growing influence that the corporations and the very wealthy have over our lives, and even our thoughts. While the Democrats tend to be a little more for the common person, in reality both parties are too much under the influence of lobbyists. The idea that our elected officials answer to lobbyists and sponsors rather than to us, the people who elected them, should have us up in arms, but it seems we are little concerned. What really is conspiring against us is our apathy, materialistic self-interest, and a lack of concern for our fellow persons.

—Bill McWhorter, Medford, 5/18/12

No. 68
Union Is Innocent

Charles Jaeger and P. Moran blamed the union for the Hostess Brands bankruptcy (Letters, Nov. 23). The true cause was vulture capitalism. The union members didn't ask for increased pay or benefits. In fact, they had already suffered layoffs and pay cuts. The company also stopped making payments to their pension fund more than a year ago. A worker with fourteen years at Hostess noted: I made $48,000 in 2005 and $34,000 last year. I would make $25,000 in five years if I took their offer. During the same period, management received increases in pay and bonuses. One CEO received a 300 percent increase in his compensation package. Instead of investing in the company, management and the private equity companies took the cash and loaded Hostess with debt. Hostess failed because of gross mismanagement and the greed of vulture capitalists. The union is innocent.

—Eric Kees, Medford, 11/12

No. 69
Stop Blaming Workers

I see from recent letters the "unions killed Twinkies" trope is alive and well in the Rogue Valley. Why we must always blame workers for our economic ills is beyond me. It is so counterintuitive to hold common working folk responsible for the misguided decisions of management and the intransigence of banks. Now, the Wall Street Journal reports that Hostess company managers stole their workers' pension contributions to use for day-to-day operations including executive bonuses while the company slid into bankruptcy. On the other hand, Hostess workers had made wage and benefit concessions over a number of years to save their jobs. It's time to stop blaming honest, hardworking Americans for the financial sins of their managers and the banks. Don't let wealthy special interests turn us against each other.

—Charles McHenry, Central Point, 11/12

No. 70
Give God a Try

The elections are over and the country is back to normal. But has anything really changed? Hope and change . . . sounds good, but unless our country is led by and its people follow the spirit of its Creator, nothing good can come from or truly be changed by the plottings of mankind. And where is the hope? "Seek ye first the Kingdom of God and every good thing will follow." Have we really given this approach a try? The evidence shows that with all of the bitterness and division seen in our recent political campaigns and with morality steadily declining as seen in our morning headlines, we haven't given it a real try. Look into ourselves too and answer "Could I be a more faithful and godly person? Now consider history. As in the days of the decadent city of Nineveh, our USA needs to reform too. Nineveh did repent, and god relented in his punishment of that city. The Lord is good and kind, slow to anger and rich in mercy. There is the hope that we're looking for. So dear friends, have hope and return to the ways of our Maker and Redeemer for his return is within our lifetime as seen by the signs of our times.

—John Mark Matson, Medford

No. 71
Pogo Was Right

A 1970 comic strip quote, "We have met the enemy and he is us," aptly describes our nation. Though we agonize over who shall serve as president, it matters little when 95 percent of our dysfunctional Congress consistently wins reelection. With minimal public debate or discussion, the Congress proved derelict in allowing President Bush or Cheney? to sacrifice American lives in the Mideast cesspool of religious zealotry. The Brown University Costs of War project estimates the actual cost of the Iraq fiasco at more than $3 trillion. Realistically, the report includes costs of caring for returning veterans through the year 2050. This $3 trillion expenditure plus another $ 600 billion expended in Afghanistan and Pakistan (to date) led to our nation's current financial predicament. During this extended period of utter waste (of American lives and dollars), Republican fiscal conservatives concentrated on tax cuts for wealthiest citizens (often themselves) while hypocritically voting to increase military expenditures. With the presidential race serving as a distraction, 95 percent of the unsavory incumbents in Congress were again reelected by Ignoramus Q. Public. Pogo was right. We are indeed the enemy.

—Robert Warren, 12/19/12

No. 72
Shootings Are a Symptom

With the recent tragic shootings, people will start talking about gun control again. But that is like treating the symptom rather than the problem. Even the shooters are but a symptom of a deeper problem: a sick society. The Bible says in Romans 1:28, "Furthermore, since they did not think it worthwhile to retain the knowledge of God, he gave them over to a depraved mind, to do what ought not to be done. They have become filled with every kind of wickedness, evil, greed and depravity. They are full of envy, murder, strife, deceit and malice." As a nation, we are now beginning to suffer the effects of turning away from God. A nation or a world without God turns into hell on earth. We think we can figure out what is wrong with us if we just work on it long enough. We will all suffer from that folly, believers along with unbelievers, as God abandons us. "The Lord is with you when you are with him. If you seek him, he will be found by you, but if you forsake him, he will forsake you" (2 Chronicles 15:2).

—Linda Hackwell, Central Point, 12/12

If any change, worthwhile, is to come about we must first recognize the problem. We live in a technological age, everything we have, everything we need is provided by technology, the taking of resources, converting them into use form, by means of the conversion of energy. To do this we of course need the resources, the knowledge to carry out the conversion and the trained person power to see that once installed it operates as it was designed.

In today's society we use money, it is the one thing not required. In actuality, it is an impedance to further progress, and in fact if its use is continued for too much longer can seriously impair our ability to survive. Most people see only symptoms, and mistakenly believe that by attacking them we will overcome our social malaise. This is a serious mistake; the problem is our antiquated social system. A system that bases its distribution of goods and services, on commodity valuation, using any form of debt token or money.

We should have a distribution system based on energy, and a system of government based on function, doing that which is necessary to bring the highest standard of living to all citizens, commensurate with the most efficient use of technology, conservation of energy, and protection of the environment. We can do no less if we are to survive and prosper.

—John C. Darvill

Quoting Howard Scott

H oward Scott, an industrial engineer, envisioned, planned, and established the organization called the Technical Alliance, the forerunner of Technocracy Inc. He, along with the extraordinary men and women selected to form the Technical Alliance, have given North America the only opportunity to understand and solve the real problems that now are threatening to engulf our area.

We present to you some of Mr. Scott's commentary on the subject of our need to dismantle our present economic and social systems, and establish a functional guidance that will allow our societies to stride into the future with assurance, rather than as presently headed, towards insecurity and chaos. His words were spoken in 1938.

Howard Scott
Founder, Director in Chief
Technocracy Inc.
1933–1970

The so-called national leadership in today's business, politics, industry and science are drenched with the putridity from the glitter of special privilege and personal aggrandizement. They shine for the moment in the immediate present, but like the dead mackerel glittering on the beach in the moonlight, the stench remains when the moonlight goes.

The function of government and business under a Price System is to maintain the values of a scarcity economy. All governmental legislation is enacted for this prime purpose.

All business practice is predicated on this premise. All disputes and disagreements will be adjudicated by the national referee of chiseling, the United States Supreme Court. Neither the federal government, nor our national business in the United States, have the structural facility, or the purpose or the desire, to abolish the economy of scarcity and to inaugurate an era of abundance. It is physically impossible for either federal government or national business, singly or collectively, to produce and distribute security and abundance in these United States.

The use of cell phones is proliferating at a tremendous rate as more people find them to be a source of immediate communication. There have been many reports linking them to possible brain tumors; these have been largely ignored, or dismissed as "not proven." Italian government researchers at the National Research Council in Bologna found that radio waves of the type emitted by cell phones, initially killed cancer cells then, after forty-eight hours, made them proliferate more rapidly. Fiorenza Marinelli, a cell biologist, exposed leukemia cells to 900 megahertz radio waves, as used by many cellular phone networks, at a power level of one milliwatt, which is between one half and ten times the power emitted by mobile phones. Initially the radiation suppressed the formation of tumors. After twenty-four hours of continuous exposure, suicide genes that prevent cancer spreading were turned on in far more leukemia cells than in cells not exposed. However after forty-eight hours' exposure he found that a survival mechanism kicked in and the cancer, briefly beaten back, became more aggressive. Three genes that trigger cells to multiply were turned on in a high proportion of the surviving cells, making them replicate ferociously. This report is from the New Scientist magazine, Marinelli said. "We don't know what the effects would be on healthy human cells, but in leukemia cells the response is always the same." "Not proven" says the industry—maybe, but by the time it is many people could have been affected. In the meantime, should we not err on the side of caution?

The Sierra Legal Defence Fund has announced that there are now only twenty-five nesting pairs of spotted owls in British Columbia, less than one hundred Vancouver Island marmots, and that the endangered orca whale is so polluted that its corpse is considered a toxic waste site. That is just a few of the 402 species listed at risk in Canada. Right across the country the number of species that are endangered is increasing every year. Still the pollution and killing goes on.

How we love our french fries! A study by Sweden's National Food Administration found high levels of acrylamide, a substance known to cause cancer in animals, in french fries. Acrylamide, a white odorless, flake-like substance, is often used in drinking water treatment and in making chemicals, dyes, and ore processing. A known carcinogen in rats, acrylamide has never been "proven" to cause cancer in humans. The researchers say an ordinary bag of potato chips may contain up to five hundred times more of the substance than the maximum allowed in drinking water by the World Health Organization. The risk seems to increase in foods that are cooked until they are brown rather than lightly done. While one order of fries won't make much difference, a lifetime probably would. Jorgen Schlundt, coordinator of the World Health Organization's food safety division, said, "The longer you eat it, the more that is in the food, the greater the risk."

California is now broke; in fact, it is more than $21 billion in debt. The California governor, Gray Davis, has declared the situation a fiscal crisis and warned there would be a sweeping package of cuts to education, health, and welfare schemes (the usual) in the next eighteen months in an attempt to balance the books. Herb Wesson, speaker of the state assembly, explained, "It's a hole so deep and so vast that even if we fired every single person on the state payroll, every park ranger, every college professor, and every Highway Patrol Officer, we would still be more than $6 billion short." State schools have been told their budgets will be cut by $3.1 billion. Mo e than thirty-five thousand teachers face being fired. Some parents are being told to give their children toilet rolls, because schools will no longer provide them. What a lovely way to run a modem technological society, with the ability to produce an abundance but unable to adequately distribute it, because of an obsolescent medium of exchange, based on money, in which fiscal manipulation takcs prcccdcncc ovcr function and efficiency, and technology is used to benefit a few, to the detriment of the many.

Its stated aim is to fight the war on terrorism, but the "Information Awareness Office of the Defense Advance Projects Agency of the Department of Defense" is far more insidious than that. Its purpose is electronic snooping on such a scale that no American citizen will be able to send or receive an e-mail, buy anything with a credit card, or make a bank deposit without it being recorded on a "virtual centralized grand database" at the Pentagon. The man in charge of this terrifying operation, one Admiral John

Poindexter, he who as Reagan's national security advisor had the idea of selling missiles to Iran, and using the proceeds to illegally support the anti-Sandinista guerillas in Nicaragua. For this he was convicted of five felonies. The purpose of the Information Awareness Office, is to know everything about everybody; its mission, it says, "is to imagine, develop, apply, integrate, demonstrate and transition apply, innate, demonstrate and transition information technologies, components and prototype, closed-loop information systems that will counter asymmetric threats by achieving total information awareness useful for preemption." Good luck interpreting that; you probably were not meant to.

Countdown to Chaos

W. C. Fields, in that wonderful nasal twang, was once quoted as saying, "There comes a time when you have to grab the bull by the tail and face the situation." He could have been talking to the people of North America today because our situation could be stated as in no bull, meaning that in regards to our virtual survival, we must reject political and business deception and confront reality.

Time is not on our side. Every year, day after day, tons of toxic residue are being dumped in and on our planet. During the year of 2001, the world's use of petroleum escalated to 28 billion barrels. That represents 1,540 trillion gallons. Not counting a plethora of additional toxins, such as pesticides, herbicides, and the general residue from industries and house hold waste, this one statist icon petroleum is phenomenal. Again, our present economies of the world, day after day, year after year, demand an ever-increasing usage of this natural resource that, by the way, is finite.

The United States, and to some extent Canada, are now in the control of personalities whose political agenda is to do whatever is necessary to further their cause without what they consider interference, i.e., the already lame checks and balances suppose d to be infused as established rules. We are marching more quickly now, down the road to fascism. We already have a well-entrenched plutocracy because our leaders are bought and paid for by the true owners of our economic system.

Politicians
The 140 of Population

One of the political maneuverings to cover the problems created by politics and business that has been very effective and profitable, is to create a war scare or actually go to war. It is "I all over again." Only this time the problems are so severe and demanding, because of ignoring or discounting the conditions in the past, that there will be no escaping them by continuing the lies and misdirection.

We are being directed to go to war to rid the world of one of the "evil ones," Saddam Hussein. He was not considered too evil when we needed him to do our bidding some years ago. He was "enthroned" with his power by some of the very people now in control of our own government. What is really going on here? Could it be that agendas are being sought that would not fit our self-serving idea of how great a nation we are? Is control of the major oil-producing countries part of the plan? If we talk of nothing else but war, will the escalating social and economic problems be concealed? And now that our economy has begun to go into a free fall, would a nice little war be the ticket to again attempt to rescue the system from collapse? Can we say for sure that these scenarios are not out of line? They certainly follow many instances of our past behavior.

However, the unending "War on Terror" cannot, for long, hold off the awareness of our economic and social system's inability to adapt to changing conditions that will create massive unemployment, retirement accounts being wiped out, and social problems such as our medical system's being near collapse.

The time is long past, but hopefully not beyond the point of no return, where we can begin to correct and change the Price System that only recognizes "making a profit," and install technocracy's functional governance that ensures that we will be making a living that will be sustainable for generations to come.

GW

The North American Technocrat (ISSN 0029-3474) is published quarterly by the North American Technocrat Messaging Board, Technocracy Inc., 2475 Harksell Road, Ferndale, WA 98248. Single copy $2.00. Yearly subscription: $6.00. Periodicals postage paid at Ferndale, WA, and additional mailing offices.

POSTMASTER: Send address changes to *The North American Technocrat*, 2475 Harksell Road, Ferndale, WA 98248.

THE NORTH AMERICAN
Technocrat

(ISSN 1540-2797) Regular Price $2.00
Fourth Quarter, 2002
Issue No. 2, Vol. 1
Ferndale, WA 98248-9764

OUR ENVIRONMENT ---
OUR ECONOMY ---
OUR SAFETY ---

ARE WE RUNNING OUT OF TIME?

The continuation and expansion of the research program and the widespread presentation of the facts is part of that task.

The growth of Technocracy has followed naturally upon the formation of common ideas based on facts. Growth by such methods has been slow but it has been a selective process that will assure a membership of the type required. People who enter an organization through emotional excitation are as readily lost to another; people who enter an organization with an understanding and acceptance of the factual basis of its program cannot be led astray. Such only are deserving of the name *Technocrat*.

The Scientific, Technological Design for the Economy of North America

Lila S. Wagner, member of Technocracy Inc.
Article reprint
The Northwest Technocrat, 1997

When we tell people that Technocracy's technological social design would solve the problems of unemployment, poverty, waste, and ecological destruction that we are experiencing today, they ask, "What is this design? Where is it? Can I see it? Can you explain it to me?" For all those questioners, one of our writers, Lila Wagner, has written this coherent explanation of the Technocracy design for a new social system.

The scientific, technological design for the economy of North America provides for:

- Complete economic security for every man, woman, and child from birth to death;
- Complete health care;
- Modem, energy-efficient housing for all;
- Education to the full extent of each individual's ability;
- Viable mass transit;
- Employment for all who are able to work and care for those who cannot; and

- Careful stewardship of the continent's natural resources and environment.

Background

As early as the winter of 1918-19, it became obvious to a group of outstanding scientists, engineers, and economists that technology was displacing man-hours of labor, leading to increased unemployment and lack of purchasing power. The group included Howard Scott, chief engineer; Frederick Ackerman, architect; Carl L. Alsberg, chemist; Allen Carpenter, MD; Stuart Chase, CPA; L. K. Comstock, electrical engineer; Alice Barrows Fernandez, educator; Bassett Jones, electrical engineer; Benton MacKaye, forester; Leland Aids, statistician; Charles P. Steinmetz, electrical engineer; Richard C. Tolman, physicist; John Carol Vaughn, MD.; Thorstein Veblen, educator; Charles H. Whitaker, housing expert; and Sullivan W. Jones, secretary.

Calling themselves the Technical Alliance, they embarked upon a survey of the energy and physical resources of the North American continent. After fourteen years of intensive study, they were able to determine that North America had the resources, both physical and energy, and the know-how, to produce an abundance for all of its citizens. What it lacked was a viable method to distribute the abundance. This inability to distribute abundance had led to a depression in 1921, the unwise introduction of installment buying in the 1920s, the stock market crash of 1929, and the Great Depression.

The Technical Alliance determined that it was the efforts to preserve the Price System, a system that had functioned, albeit imperfectly, during the centuries of scarcity, that had led to the denouement of the '30s. They saw that a system that had grown out of conditions of scarcity could not function adequately to distribute abundance.

Requirements to Be Met

A system which could distribute abundance and satisfy the conditions listed above would need these features:

1. It must register continuously the energy converted in the total day-to-day operation of the continent, both plant construction and maintenance, as well as the energy converted in the production of goods and services for personal consumption by the population.
2. By registering the energy converted, it would be possible to maintain a continuous inventory and to balance production with consumption, eliminating both scarcity of any one commodity and unnecessary resource depletion due to overproduction of some other.
3. This inventory could provide information as to the type of goods and services produced, where and how much had been used in order to give replacement information, and could, if desired, identify the user.
4. It must distribute goods and services to every member of the population, giving each individual citizen the widest possible choice in consuming his share of the continental physical wealth.
5. It must guarantee that each individual's consuming power be his, or hers, alone, much as a social security number is assigned to each individual, and is not to be transferred to anyone else.

What Would Be the Means of Distribution?

On each of these counts, money fails to meet the requirement for distributing abundance.

- It is not a measure of energy converted, or of production or consumption of goods and services.
- It can be transferred from one person to another, a fact which could deprive some citizens of their share of abundance, besides making fraud and bribery possible.
- It can be stashed away. In this connection it must be noted that any objection in a flow line, even at the consuming

end, will eventually shut the line down; money will not keep production moving evenly.

On all counts, money does not meet the requirements of a medium of distribution of abundance.

The mechanism that does meet the requirements is the energy degraded in the production of goods and services. This energy loss constitutes the physical cost of production and can be stated in units of work (ergs or kwh) or in units of heat (kg calories or BTUs). We can, therefore, measure quite accurately the energy lost in any given industrial process, as well as the total physical cost of operating the continent.

After subtracting the energy required to operate the continent as a whole-new plant and maintenance thereof, roads, housing, schools, local transport, continental transport, communications, education, child care, and maintenance of public institutions-the remainder would be shared equally by all adult citizens in the form of personal energy credits. In the US alone, in 1992, more than 81 quadrillion BTUs were consumed, with 62 quadrillion being used for overall operating, leaving 19 quadrillion to be consumed by the personal needs of the population. That should supply every North American with his favorite personal items, all else being supplied as a right of citizenship.

Keep in mind: to be consumed. Since there is a definite limit to the amount of goods and services one individual can consume, it is both reasonable and efficient to issue equal numbers of personal energy units to each adult, male and female alike. It is anticipated that the number will be greater than anyone can reasonably use before the units expire, at which time new units would be issued. These energy credits would be usable only by the person to whom they are issued; no one else could "cash" them. Since everyone would have his own plentiful supply, there would be no point in transferring credits to any other person—or stealing someone else's!

How Will Society Be Organized in a Technate?

First, realize that it will take years, even decades, to overcome the thought-patterns and habits that have been the norm in the Price System. The urge to acquire things in order to gain recognition must give to a desire to excel in one's chosen field of endeavor. Whole new complexes of energy-efficient housing interspersed with green areas and local cultural facilities must take the place of the millions of units of substandard housing and the decaying infrastructure which exist today. Taxes and monetary debt will be unknown. Crimes involving property—95 percent of all crime—will no longer be a problem. Disparity between rich and poor will vanish and, with it, eventually, racism, sexism, classism, ageism—most of today's troubles.

Can we do a global makeover? Not until we have put our own house (read Continent) in order. To bite off more than we can chew is a sure prescription for failure. When things are running smoothly in North America, then we can invite young people from other countries to come and observe what can be adapted to their situation.

After the period of transition is over, the children born into the Technate will enjoy lifetime economic security and education to age twenty-five, as a right of citizenship. At twenty-five, after being exposed to the many careers available, they will choose the one best suited to their talents for their life's work—a work life that will last probably twenty years of four-day weeks of four-hour days with seventy-eight days' continuous vacation each year. At about age forty-five, then, they will retire at full compensation, free to travel, enjoy a hobby, study, whatever.

The actual operation of the Technate will continue as society operates today—those with the expertise in the various lines of industry and the professions will carry on all necessary functions. We will be well

Technocracy stands ready to try to help ease the birth pangs if, indeed, a new social order is to be born.

—John Sheldon

A New Approach

By Dean Cameron
Member of Technocracy Inc.

The building of a new social order on the North American continent demands an entirely new technique of organization. Technocracy is working toward the definite objective of a new social order of abundance and security for all—an objective that is predetermined by the very structure of our continental physical mechanism. A thorough study of the current progression of North America indicates that nothing short of this objective will satisfy the needs of our people or the operating specifications of our technology. This is not a matter for compromise, as some suggest, in an effort to modify, reform, or confine the present outmoded method of social control. It is a gigantic problem-as large as all North America and the full impact of modem technology—and it cannot be solved by a compromise of agreement among many diverse opinions. This is a problem that can only be solved by the design and installation of a new social order. Such demands a new form of organization.

In most instances, individuals join in voluntary association to act upon those opinions, ideas, or beliefs which they hold in common. These opinions, ideas, or beliefs may or may not be in accord with facts, although group action may and does take place in entire disregard to facts—often with disastrous results. Once ideas have crystallized into organized action, little question is raised or permitted as to their feasibility or conformance to fact. In these cases-the union of men of widely differing conditioning with a consequent wide range of opinion, ideas, or beliefs-it often follows that the objective of the group is either initially or ultimately the result of compromise, or is, of necessity extremely limited or general in scope. This explains the popularity and ineffectiveness of the emotional approach and the political generality neither clearly states nor adequately defines the project—both are readily adapted by the individual to his existing stock of ideas.

Technocracy partakes of only one of these elements in that it is dependent on the voluntary association of individuals acting upon certain ideas upon which they are in agreement. It differs, however, from all other social movements past and present, in that these common ideas are not the result of philosophic agreement. Compromise, in so far as it may enter into the building of this organization, must be entirely upon the part of the individual in allying himself with the movement.

It will be seen that the building of such a movement demands an approach that is a direct inversion of the methods employed by all other social movements. The emotional popularization of Technocracy's program would mean but a temporary gain; persons drawn into a movement by such means are good only for immediate action-rarely can they be held for a long-term program. This is amply illustrated by the rapid growth and decay of the many contemporary social movements that have employed such methods. Technocracy's task is one of providing facts, facts upon which all may build common ideas.

THE ECOLOGY OF MAN

North America can no longer be occupied by a high-energy
civilization operated on a haphazard, planless basis.
We must plan for survival!
Technocracy Inc.
Ferndale, WA
www.technocracyinc.org

From *The Technocrat* magazine,
vol. 16, no. 12 (copyright 1948).

Technocracy has always insisted that the type of social operation it offers is not just desirable; it is necessary. As we peruse this pamphlet, we ask ourselves the question "Can man continue to live at all on this continent without drastically changing his methods of management?"

The Ecology of Man

This is not a pleasant pamphlet to read. It will frighten the reader into realizing just how close to the edge our blundering Price System has led us, and how casually our ignorant political and financial leaders are ignoring the facts of life. It is this persistent refusal to face facts that has been the cause of all our difficulties as a nation in the past thirty years.

Ecology is the study of organisms in relation to their environment. Since no one organism lives strictly to itself, the study of ecology involves the interrelationships of many organisms as well as the relationships of these organisms with the nonorganic environment.

The Web of Life

This complex is often spoken of as the web of life. The principal components of the environment are plants, animals, minerals, and water, with other factors of varying importance, which we shall omit from our present discussion.

When there is an essential stability in the environment, that is, when conditions and relationships do not change much from year to year, we speak of it as the balance of nature. When there is a stabilized, dynamic balance between plants, animals, minerals, and water, a particular and interesting condition prevails-the return of ingredients to the environment from year to year is essentially equal to that which is removed.

For example, the plants and animals which die are replaced by similar plants and animals. No more water is removed than what accumulates during the year. Fertility which is taken from the soil is restored. Under such conditions, and excepting a major geological change, the prevailing environment could be maintained for an indefinite period of time.

The balance of nature is often upset, however. A whole area may be affected by a geological change, such as change of climate (temperature and humidity) or change of elevation or topography. A local upset of much smaller magnitude occurs when an area is burned over or is invaded by a sand dune or a volcanic deposit.

Following events which wipe out all, or most of life, a period of rehabitation must occur. The first life that comes into an area is called the pioneer flora and fauna. The pioneer life is only temporary; it is soon replaced by other kinds of life once a suitable environment is prepared for them. These in turn are followed by still other forms. Thus, there is a succession of life-a series of changes in the organic components of the environment, in which transitional species successively come into prominence, only to fade out of the scene.

Eventually, a new balance is established which is again stable. The final association of plants and animals in an ecological succession is known as the climax association. It tends to be stable for a long period of time.

We might use a burned-over forest area as an example for further illustration. In this case, the pioneer species of plants would probably be various types of herbs, the kind depending upon the geographical locality, the humidity, and the elevation. These will not remain long as the dominant species, but will soon have that position usurped by other species-probably various kinds of shrubs. These will probably be replaced by trees, and these first trees by other kinds of trees.

Eventually, a climax flora will become established which is permanent. This flora, and the fauna which is associated with it, constitute a balanced association, not only between the component organisms, but also with the water supply and the minerals of that area. However, it may take many years for the transitional changes to result in the climax association. But this climax association may not be composed of the same types of plants and animals as the one that prevailed before the fire. The main thing of importance is that the association is in balance and it is able to maintain itself in the face of other organic competition for that area.

Man Now Dominant Species

Among the ecological associations of the world, man is now the most dominant species of animal, except in a few areas where he has not penetrated in large numbers. Although man has been a component part of the world's balance of nature, it was not until quite recently in his history that he became a disturbing influence to that balance. Because of his greater innate intelligence and his inventiveness, as well as his social organization, man was able to tilt the dynamic balance more and more in his favor.

The invention of weapons and tools, the use of fire, and the development of language (as a means of communication and social memory) gave man a decided advantage in the struggle for survival over other animals of comparable or even larger size. The domestication of plants and animals and other technological developments accelerated this advantage through the centuries, until now man has become almost everywhere the most dominant species in the environment, if not in numbers, at least in the effect which he has produced.

During 98 percent of man's 7,000 years of civilized existence on the earth, this technological progress was so slow that the disturbance of the general ecological balance was only of a minor magnitude and only local in its effects. But the last 2 percent of that time—the last 140 years—tells a far different story. During this time, man has become a plague upon the earth. He has exterminated or exhausted many species which once roamed the earth, flew the sky, or swam the waters by the hundreds of millions. He has plowed up the sod and slashed away at the plant growth, until many areas which were once verdant with forests and grass are now desolate. The ecological environment in which man as a species could flourish is now shrinking because of his own careless behavior.

Man has also let his population increase to the point where it has become self-destructive. He must not only combat the other elements of the environment in order to survive, but he must battle within his own species to determine which individuals and which groups are to survive. No matter how one tries to rationalize the value of human life, one cannot escape the conclusion that there are just too many human beings on the earth.

As a result of this overburden of human population, the destruction of forests and other organic life which is consumed in the processes of human living is in many instances greater than the replacement of the particular species involved. Overgrazing of the rangelands in the western United States, for example, has so reduced the edible plants and so eroded the soil that the rangelands will not support more than a fraction of the livestock that they did fifty or more years ago. The people of North America are cutting off the forests faster than they are being replenished. Even certain species of life in the ocean are becoming exhausted, not only the great whales, but certain species of shellfish and true fishes used for food.

Man Endangers His Environment

It is not only these organic factors of the environment that are being disturbed by man's recent activities on the earth, but the disturbance extends into the inorganic elements as well. Among these is groundwater. Through millions of years, the rocks of the earth have been saturated with water below a certain level. This level is known as the water table. Man has disturbed this ground in a great many places. He has instituted drainage to remove surplus water from the surface, which has resulted in a lowering of the water table. He has destroyed the plant cover in many places and this permits a more rapid runoff, hence less water seeps into the ground. He has drilled wells and pumped the water out of the ground at a faster rate than it is replaced by natural means. He has diverted many lakes, streams, and underground flows into the water mains of his large cities and then increased the population of the cities beyond the capacities of the water to supply their needs. Thus, in many areas where there was adequate water to supply a moderate population on a long-term basis, there is now a deficiency of water because of the uncontrolled increase of the population and the shortsighted exploitation of the water resources.

Another inorganic factor which man is misusing is the arable soil of the earth. It is estimated that about a fourth of the original arable soil area of the earth has been ruined, with a large part of the remainder damaged. On the basis of the factor of suitable land area alone, there are already six hundred million more people on the earth than the soil can feed with a decent diet. But the population is increasing at the rate of more than twenty million a year and the acreage of productive soil is declining.

But, these are not the most critical factors affecting man's ecological balance. During his industrial growth, accompanied by the wasteful practices of business exploitation, man has become ravenous in the use of many minerals, ranging from iron ore to phosphate fertilizers. A number of the most critical of these minerals are nearing the stage of deficiency and some are rapidly approaching exhaustion. For example, the United States can no longer supply all of its own present consumption of copper, lead, zinc, tungsten, manganese, and petroleum. The United States is importing all of these to meet its domestic demands. Iron ore will soon be added to this list.

It is of little moment, in the long run, whether the human species on this continent can maintain its present industrial pace for another ten years or another hundred. In reviewing the overall picture, we have neglected the details which support the general conclusions, but the details are there in abundance.

The important thing we are attempting here is a long-range projection of man's ecological trend, especially as it pertains to the North American continent. This much we can say for sure: man will not be able to live on the North American continent for the next generation as he has lived for the past generation. He has been too prodigal with his heritage. This has left him in the position of being repudiated by his environment.

The people of North America cannot continue, for even a few more years, their present magnitude of free-enterprise operations.

The environment will not supply the raw materials for this type of human onslaught for long. What the future of the people now living on the continent will become is something fearful to contemplate. Yet, the North American citizen, instead of acknowledging the facts and recognizing the trend, is blindly and blatantly going ahead to increase the rate of the very factors which are contributing most toward the downfall of his vaunted civilization.

Man under his present mode of operation is not a climax species in the environment. He is a transitional species, for he is taking more from the environment than is being replaced. He is scheduled, therefore, in the course of events to lose his dominant position in the organic association, perhaps, to be superseded as the number one species by something else. Whether that something is insect, rodent, or weed does not much matter to us, once man succumbs.

The same factors that are pointing in a downward direction here on North America also apply to a greater or lesser degree to other parts of the world. In summary, they are these: excessive population, soil erosion and depletion, destruction of forests and rangelands, excessive use of groundwater, and exhaustion of vital mineral deposits.

To the student of trends, the future of the human race on the earth appears dismal. The most dismal aspect is the apathy toward or the flagrant denial of this trend by our so-called leaders. Businessmen and politicians are clamoring for a more rapid acceleration of the very trends which are in force. These two groups of social traitors are even contemplating a third world war—the greatest of them all—although everybody who understands anything about it warns that such a catastrophe would deplete the very resources on which our industrial civilization and "high standard" of living depend.

A few students of human affairs recognize what is happening and make a fairly accurate analysis of the situation. Their descriptions are clear, their analyses of the prevailing trends and appraisals of the danger leave no doubt as to the probability of dire consequences, and their warnings are almost hysterical. But when it comes to giving a synthesis for survival, most of their suggestions are puerile or fantastic; they lack the realism and boldness of concept which the analysis demands.

Typical of this type of literature is William Vogt's book Road to Survival. The author draws a very clear picture of the perils facing human civilization and gives some of the basic causes. His descriptions are vivid, his analysis is good, but his synthesis is pathetic. In the early part of the book he tells the story of a Chinese man by the name of Wong. Wong and his family are starving; so, Wong goes forth to see if somewhere he can scrape up something to eat. Meeting with repeated failure, Wong finally gives up and sits down to die.

William Vogt is in some ways like Wong. He studies the situation, sees the facts, points out the trends, indicates in general what must be done; but, when he looks into the future, he sees little hope. After making a few puerile gestures toward a synthesis, he tosses the problem into the "lap of the gods" and, intellectually speaking, sits down to die. Vogt states that the program must have three parts: "research, education, and action on the land." He realizes that such a program must be organized, but does not know how it should be organized; he pleads incompetence, and expresses the hope that the United Nations will somehow acquire the vision and the unity needed to handle the job. He hates large technological operations (such as the Tennessee Valley Authority) and centralized industries; he wants to see some sort of a retrogressive trend toward small-scale operation. He wants a program of birth control, one that is voluntary and which does not offend anybody or any institution. He proclaims his faith in democracy and recommends that we prepare to "pull in our belts and accept a long period of austerity." He hopes that if the dilemma is made known to all mankind, that somehow the people will see the light. Then he concludes:

Unless we take these steps and begin to swing into them soon—unless in short, man readjusts his way of living, in its fullest sense, to the imperatives imposed by the limited resources of his environment-we may as well give up all hope of continuing civilized life. Like Gadarene swine, we shall rush down a war-torn slope to a barbarian existence in the blackened rubble.

It is a sad commentary on the intelligence of the human species that it is not able to plan adequately for its own survival. Now that civilized man has become dominant in the organic world and has every advantage, it seems paradoxical that he should be headed pell-mell for oblivion.

Technocracy Proposes

The picture might, indeed, be as dark as William Vogt paints it, except for the thinking of one man. One man had the intelligence, the strategical genius, and the integrity to develop an idea for human survival that is in harmony with the facts and with the social needs of man. At times almost single-handed, this man Howard Scott worked out a strategy of social operations that could be blueprinted into a social plan for the North American continent. This idea, in time, became known as Technocracy.

But, Technocracy was not a popular program. If man was to survive, he would have to change many of his ways; he would have to abandon his concepts of individual anarchy, also, he would have to repudiate his politics, his business enterprises, and his uncontrolled wastage of natural resources. This did not set well with the people of North America; it did not cater to their soft, sentimental illusions. It made many enemies and it faced a stone wall of human inertia. It was not an idea that could win popular acceptance and support overnight. It was an idea that would have to penetrate slowly into the social intelligence of the people; but, it was an idea that had to grow and expand, for its time had come. It could not be denied for long.

Technocracy is today the only refutation of the prediction that man's civilization is doomed to failure. Technocracy maintains that it is possible for man to remain the dominant species on earth and at the same time enjoy a high standard of living for many centuries to come. It is possible for him to be the climax species in a new ecological balance, and it is possible for him to do this at a level of existence even far above that of the average North American of today. It has the only blueprint for a high-energy social mechanism that will not run down.

To do this, man must adopt a new strategy for his social operations and change his mode of living to conform to that strategy. He must return unto the ecological system as much as he takes from it. If man can do that, he can survive and flourish for thousands of years more on earth. If he does not do it, nature will take a ruthless course so far as the human species is concerned.

Technocracy's blueprint pertains specifically to North America as an operational unit. If the world is ever to install a scientific social control it must begin somewhere. The reasons why Technocracy selects North America as the beginning place are two: (1) North America happens to be where the idea of Technocracy originated; it is the home of the Technocrats; (2) North America is the easiest place on which to install such an operation.

This does not mean Technocrats ignore the rest of the world completely; rather, they have a serious concern for all areas of the earth. It is possible that eventually Technocracy will be introduced and installed on other continents, but it must be established in some one place first. It cannot be done everywhere at once. The most unfavorable parts of the world will have to be left in a state of virtual abandonment until more favorable areas are set up and operating.

We do not wish to imply by the foregoing that Technocracy Inc. has a world program. We are merely making a long-range speculation for the future of an idea. Technocracy's only blueprint program is for North America. When Technocracy is well established here, that will be the time for us more seriously to contemplate the endemic problems of other parts of the earth. Technocracy is a forceful and realistic program with a superb strategy in support of human survival and advancement. It is not a weak philosophical dream, infected with the virus of a wishful-thinking goodwill. It is a program with concept stern enough to get the job done. It is as uncompromising as the grim question which must be answered soon—the question of survival.

Man's existence under the Price System is transitional, for the Price System does not provide the strategy for a long-term survival. It only offers man a chance to reap a quick profit and move on. The bonanza of Price System enterprise is even now running into borasca. A new concept and a new pattern of economic living is mandatory for the future if man's ecological position is to be to his liking. That concept and that pattern cannot be found within the framework of the Price System. That means that North Americans cannot go on doing for long what they are now doing. They can adhere stubbornly to the concepts of the status quo and blunder into catastrophe, or they can accept the planned progression outlined by Howard Scott and advance upward into the future. Technocracy is prepared to show the way.

In order to continue at a high level of civilization for an indefinite period of time, North Americans must do these things:

They must conserve the fresh water of the continent and return it to the ground in such a way as to build up the water table and maintain it at as favorable a level as possible. This can be done most effectively through the Continental Hydrology Program designed by Technocracy. This program provides for the maximum use of the fresh water resources of the continent on a balanced basis.

They must return to the soil the fertility which is taken from it in the process of raising plants and animals. For the most part, this means that the fertility must never leave the soil area. We cannot depend indefinitely on scarce deposits of mineral fertilizer to make up for the wasteful depletion of the natural fertility. Such a program demands a continental agrobiology, scientifically designed, wherein the plant and animal crop of the continent will provide an abundance of food for the population and products for the industries of the continent, without depleting the productivity of the soil. Only Technocracy can furnish the strategy necessary to the solution of that problem.

They must be careful in their use of the non-replaceable mineral resources of the continent. More abundant materials should be used wherever possible in place of scarce materials and replaceable materials used in place of non-replaceable materials. Then a program of maximum use and maximum recovery must be instituted. We cannot afford, for example, to discard forty-eight billion metal cans and twenty-six billion bottles on the national trash piles each year, nor be lavish in the use of lead as a basic ingredient for paint. This program can be carried out, but not under the Price System. We must turn again to Technocracy for the answer.

They must establish a balanced utilization of energy. We cannot plan to operate for long on fossil fuel as our major energy source. Instead, we must adopt a system of energy use which will obtain a maximum amount of energy from renewable sources and a minimum amount from nonrenewable sources. Technocracy's program provides for such an energy balance. The Price System on the other hand refuses to face the problem, but seeks to deplete our limited fossil fuels at the maximum rate that will yield a "fair return" in the way of profits.

They must institute a program of population control which will keep the population within the bounds of the long-range capacity of food, water, minerals and energy supplies. North America is not seriously overburdened with population at present, but it is gradually approaching that condition. The population of North America should not much exceed two hundred million. No political party can touch these problems concerning the population, but science can find a ready answer.

We have here presented the problem of North America in bare outline. And we have pointed out some of the goals that must be reached. But it is evident that the problem will not solve itself—at least not in any way that we will like. It can only be solved by an intentional and coordinated effort on the part of North American citizens to get it solved. They must be the ones who execute the tactics which support the strategy for survival.

The Price System does not have any strategy for survival; it does not even have the mechanism by which an effective strategy can be implemented. In the long run, the operations of the Price System are defeatist. The Price System can only mine out the resources and move on. When the resources are gone—what then? Well, that day is rushing upon us. Our technological development has given it a momentum that it never had before. This generation must face the problem and find the answer.

Technocracy has always pointed out that Technocracy's method of social operation will not be adopted because it is desirable, but because it is necessary. The choice is literally between Technocracy and chaos.

Science applied to the social order is the only effective technique of doing this. This is the method of Technocracy. Science has never yet let the human race down; business and politics have never done otherwise. Technocracy is nonbusiness and nonpolitical—it is strictly scientific. It alone can meet the requirements.

As painful as it may be to you, you must make a decision. The march of events will not let you sit on a fence or equivocate for long. So, you might as well decide now. Which are you for—the "blundercats" of the Price System, or the Technocrats? No matter how smart you are in the immediate manipulations of the moment, you have no security under "blunderocracy." The only future worthwhile is a future in Technocracy.

You do not have to be a genius to be a Technocrat. But you must have integrity and an attitude of cooperative endeavor. You must be prepared to function as an integral part of a self-disciplined body of people with a definite social objective. In Technocracy, there are many "little" jobs to be done which are as important as the so-called bigjobs. In Technocracy, there is no place for individual anarchy, ego inflation, or opinionation. But there is plenty of room for function, and it is function that will get the job done. There is no material reward and no glory beyond the satisfaction of doing what must be done.

For all who can qualify on this basis, there is room and a job in Technocracy. Can you qualify?

—Wilton Ivie

Published by Continental Headquarters, Technocracy Inc., 44874
Member at large Ferndale, WA
Edmond D. Vongehr
www.technocracyinc.org
571-661-5325

To All Interested Parties

September 14, 2001

As a World War II volunteer veteran with 500 hours' experience in B-24s and fifty years as a self-employed businessman, I feel it is my duty as a loyal American citizen to make the following statement:

Questions? Should we elect and put in power men who have enormous wealth to make decisions for the average American family who cares very little what happens in the rest of the world?

The average man and woman's energies and thoughts are consumed in making a living and paying their bills to survive. The politician with the most money usually wins the elections.

Money, they say, is the root of all evil. Should we not blame our rich politicians and leaders for the world hating America? When our leaders and their associates have financial interests in the countries that are being bombed and innocent women and children are being killed, is this not a conflict of interest? Retaliation can be evil, as we have seen. But do we now allow our leaders to retaliate?

Would that not cause more retaliation from both sides? Are we the American people being duped into allowing this conflict of interest?

Money and greed are powerful instincts. Evil breeds evil. Christ said, "Tum the other cheek." Can you and I?

Most Americans can't understand why other people of the world hate us. The average American is unaware how our leaders deal with other countries and their leaders.

Now, the big question? Are we being prepared by our leaders, through panic, hysteria, and fear to retaliate against unknown forces that could start the beginning of the end for life as we know it? I don't believe this is the time to stir up emotions and hatred with threats of vengeance when we do not know for sure who even caused the disaster to our people.

Don't we need sober, patient, intelligent, and coolheaded leadership to make decisions affecting the lives of all Americans and other innocent people all over the world, especially at this crucial time in history?

I think every one of us knows the USA is one of the strongest powers in the world and has the armies, navies, and air force to blow the world apart many times. Other nations also have that power, plus the fact it has been proven volunteers can penetrate our borders, and cause tremendous damage in our cities and countrysides through guerrilla warfare.

And this can happen. One of our past presidents stated, "Talk softly but carry a big stick." We carry the big stick, but our politicians are not talking softly. They are pounding their chests and telling the world what they are going to do to retaliate, voting into law forty billion us dollars for war funds to start the war.

If they have to stand before the cameras and tell the American people and the rest of the people in the world, how cruelty has come to American people, could they not speak softly and reverently and sadly, at least for a period laid aside for mourning?

Sadly,
E. D. Vongehr

Something New Under the Sun

Technocracy—new, startling, fundamental-has invaded the minds of North Americans with unparalleled positiveness and force.

Its original research summary, a simple statement of facts about the critical period in which we find ourselves, startled the world. The questions it posed still remain unanswered.

Technocracy not only made the American people "fact conscious" but confronted the entire continent with the inevitability of fundamental social change.

Technocracy's position is based on facts, not rhetoric. Its message has cut deep. It has reached more intelligent and functionally important citizens in all walks of life than any other organization, and continues to do so.

Technocracy's scientific approach to the social problem is unique, and its method is completely new. It speaks the language of science, and recognizes no authority but the facts.

In Technology we see science banishing waste, unemployment, hunger, and insecurity of income forever.

In Technocracy we see science replacing an economy of scarcity with era of abundance.

In Technocracy we see functional competence displacing grotesque and wasteful incompetence, facts displacing guesswork, order displacing disorder, industrial planning displacing industrial chaos.

Technocracy is the extension of science to build a civilization worthy of the intelligence of man.

Technocracy concerns itself with the continental area of North America alone. Technocracy marks a turning point in American history-the birth of a greater America. Technocracy contains all the elements out of which great movements are made.

www.technocracyinc.org

Technocracy Inc.

Information Brief
Number 73

The most dangerous threats to human existence today are the population explosion and the deterioration of the physical environment. They are interrelated, and both are the result of widespread ignorance and indifference by man himself. Man's continued existence depends on science, technology, and intelligent care of the physical environment. No longer can man live by the primitive methods of his forefathers, nor can he continue to live by the careless exploitation of the world's ecology.

Some progress is being made toward informing the citizens of this continent concerning their environment. However, seldom are the many environmental problems being added up so that they can understand the total disaster now approaching, or the total requirements for its correction or the total dangers of the failure to do so.

The world's population is increasing at the rate of ninety million per year, forests are being destroyed, soil is eroding, and mineral resources are being exhausted. Hazardous wastes are accumulating for which no safe disposal has been arranged. Land, sea, and air are being polluted to dangerous levels, the ozone layer is being depleted, and greenhouse gases are being added to the atmosphere at an accelerating rate. Under these conditions, man is not a permanent resident of this earth. He is a temporary species. For he is taking more from the environment than is being replaced.

It is a sad commentary on the intelligence of the human species that it is not able to plan adequately for its own survival. Now that civilized man has become dominant in the organic world, it seems paradoxical that he should be headed pell-mell for oblivion.

To a student of trends, the future of the human species on this earth appears dismal. Worst of all is the apathy and flagrant denial of these trends by our so-called leaders who are clamoring for a more rapid acceleration of the very trends which cause the problems. All the promises made by politicians are useless drivel. Only adequate planning followed by competent action can provide effective solutions.

In order to continue at a high level of civilization for an extended period of time, North Americans must accept the changes required:

- They must establish a balanced utilization of energy.
- They must return to the soil the fertility which is taken from it.
- They must conserve the continent's fresh water and mineral resources.
- They must institute a program of population control.
- They must discontinue the depletion of the ozone layer.
- They must slow down the buildup of gases which cause acid rain and gases which may produce a greenhouse effect.
- And, most difficult of all, they must eliminate the monetary motivation which prohibits the above requirements from being accomplished.

These things need doing under any circumstances, and they certainly must be done if the human species is to continue living on this planet. To do this, man must adopt a new strategy for his social operations and change his mode of living to conform to that strategy. He must return unto the ecological system as much as he takes from it. If man can do this, he can survive and flourish for thousands of years more on earth. If he does not do it, nature will take a ruthless course so far as the human species is concerned.

Many of the world's environmental problems are global in scope. The winds blow pollution across national boundaries, and the Chernobyl disaster demonstrated the international dangers of nuclear radiation. Furthermore, as industrial nations continue to deplete their own natural resources, they become increasingly dependent on imports from other countries. Solutions to such global problems must be on a worldwide basis. However, the solutions have to start somewhere. Some nation or continent must lead the way. North America has the best qualifications for this leadership if its people can overcome their own politico/economic interference. But only after this continent has solved its own problems can it be effective in providing leadership for other nations.

How can a government which is $3 trillion in debt provide the trillions required to assist other countries? How can it repair its own infrastructure, finance environmental clean-ups, bail out its savings and loans, wipe out its own poverty and homelessness, and eliminate the drug problem without a collapse of its economic structure?

How can a nation which can't solve the problem of poverty in the midst of plenty in its own country provide solutions for the world's problems? North America's economic system must be totally redesigned from top to bottom. This Price System of scarcity values "just grew" long before the technological age and long before there were major environmental problems. The order of magnitude of the highly technical operations that are required is far beyond the economic abilities of a Price System.

More than a half century ago, Technocracy Inc. first stated that a time would come when the Price System would become inoperable. This means that the country's increasing problems would become so severe that they couldn't be solved by Price System methods. As a result of its study, Technocracy has designed the only Technological Social Design in existence. It is the only method available which can replace the Price System. This new design is offered to the North American people as a gift. May we soon demonstrate the intelligence to accept it.

The time for decision has arrived.

Or Section Stamp

Technocracy

Technocracy originated in the winter of 1918–1919 when Howard Scott formed a group of scientists, engineers, and economists that became known in 1920 as the Technical Alliance—a research organization. In 1933, it was incorporated under the laws of the State of New York as a nonprofit, nonpolitical, nonsectarian membership organization. It has no affiliation with any other organization, group, or association either in North America or elsewhere.

Health problems result from environmental degradation, they are partially recovered by doctor and hospital bills. When a building must be repainted because acid rain has damaged the paint, some of the costs are "recovered" by painters and paint manufacturers. All this adds a bit to the number of jobs for people.

However, only a small fraction of the total costs of environmental deterioration is recovered in this manner. Much of the cost is postponed to some future date. For example, consider the time when the earth's oil is depleted to uneconomic levels, what will the cost be to solve this problem? When there is no longer enough arable soil to support a continued expansion of population levels, and starvation increases accordingly, will there be a way to pay, in money, for this? Will it be paid by adding to the present debt? Or will it be paid for by the loss of life required to bring population levels into balance with the ability of the earth's resources to support them? Or will it be some combination of both?

There have been some important and successful efforts made on behalf of the environment. However, these successes have been rendered far less effective by the rapid population increase. Further, they have become less effective as some people find their bread better buttered with money if they work against such projects. Obviously, integrity and intestinal fortitude are both required to be an honest environmentalist.

Scientists are humans with the same desires, human needs, and ego problems as anyone else. The difference is that they have been trained to accept verifiable information, at least in their own field of expertise. Environmental scientists, for example, have carefully investigated the ecological conditions in which mankind must live. Much is yet to be learned, but much has already been learned. The book Road to Survival by William Vogt, and The Ecology of Man by Wilton Ivie, both published in 1948, are proof that this field of science is at least fifty years old. Environmental scientists do not claim that they are always correct, but since their work is always subject to review by other scientists, the chance of their accuracy is far greater than that of any other group or individual.

We would do well to investigate the motives of lobbyists and politicians who try to lull the public into believing that environmental conditions are not approaching a danger point. We may find that such attempts may prove to be social treason.

What are the changes necessary for the survival of the human species?

1. Population growth must be reversed and become a negative growth.
2. A balance between population and the earth's ability to supply human needs on a long-range basis must be achieved.
3. The physical environment must be conserved for the benefit of future generations.
4. The citizens of this continent (and elsewhere) must make a serious effort to learn to select a leadership which has some understanding of the physical requirements of life and how they can be provided.
5. The monetary motivation, which provides the incentive for an ever more rapid destruction of the environment, must be replaced by methods which provide the incentive for conservation.

Number 5 is, perhaps, the most difficult of all the necessary requirements for human survival. It will require the most widespread use of the greatest number of intelligent people of any social change in human history. At this point in history, it is quite uncertain that this human characteristic is present in sufficient quantities. It certainly wasn't during the 1930s depression when it was so obvious that something was seriously out of balance-when food was destroyed while people were hungry. (We still do this.)

To further complicate matters, a point of no return could be reached in environmental deterioration beyond which the condition could never be corrected. With present exponential growth in so many areas now reaching impossible heights, this could happen very quickly, and perhaps, without recognition until too late.

There can be no hope for the future of the human species if so many people continue to refuse to consider the environmental and economic deterioration now in progress. The world desperately needs some country, or continent, to solve its physical and economic problems in order to set an example for others to follow. To date, no such example exists.

Here we are, a species threatened with extinction, or very close to it, hurtling headlong, full steam ahead, with little purpose except to make money. How sad it is that future historians, if any, must record the breakdown of the nearest thing to a civilization yet to exist on this earth, because of a shortage of intestinal fortitude.

L. W. Nicholson
Member of Technocracy
26 Center St., Travelers Rest, SC 29690
Phone: 864-834-1664

Technocracy to the Rescue

"A Famous Novelist Hails the Technocrats' Vision of a Happy World Governed by Engineering Skill," *Liberty Magazine*, February 18, 1933, by Rupert Hughes

Whenever something new is offered to the world as a cure for old diseases, it is misrepresented by everybody concerned. The inventor or discoverer, like Archimedes, leaps out of the inspiring bathtub, cries "Eureka!" and runs, all wet, down the street, proclaiming the great godsend. Then friends and converts take the hopes and dreams of the inventor and magnify them, twist them, and vouch for them as cure-alls. Then the enemies of all new things take alarm and begin to attack something that the inventor never claimed and his partisans never pretended.

Everybody makes mistakes in figures, but on catching somebody else in a typographical or mathematical error, thinks he has finished him. When Sir Isaac Newton discovered the law of gravity and tried to verify it, the great mathematician was so excited that he had to call in a friend to do a simple bit of addition. Yet Newton has a good name and the law was a good thing to learn.

So it is with Technocracy, as I see it. It is a magnificent theory, a branch of the theory of evolution and as easy to misrepresent and get mad at; some of its first disciples have been extremely rash and prophetic, and its enemies are ridiculing those follies and committing new follies of their own. I believe that, in its essence, it is a true statement of irresistible tendencies. Before we can find a cure, we need a diagnosis. This being correct or corrected, there is still much room for error in the prophecy or prognosis. But somewhere, somehow, in a certain general direction, something waits to be done.

Technocracy means "government by skill"; skill means wisdom based on knowledge, knowing how to do things, especially with tools, implements, machines, scientific devices, neat tricks. Technocracy concerns the management of the physical work of the world. It has nothing to do with the control of the fine arts, religions, philosophies, jokes, amusements, and fashions.

Can anyone object to a rule of the world by skill? Is it not high time that we had a bit of it?

We have had aristocracy, autocracy, bureaucracy, democracy, Technocracy, plutocracy, theocracy, hierarchy, monarchy—all the archies and cracies of kings, priests, the wise and good, the mob, the pee-pul—which means the politicians "representing" the people. And, today, all forms of government are stuck in the mud, together.

And now comes along a suggestion that we let skill run the world. The idea is backed up with a warning that the machine which man has invented will serve as a juggernaut if allowed to run wild, but will serve as a magnificent omnibus if only everybody will get aboard and ride, each one taking his spell at the wheel or other parts of the machinery. Technocracy is really a trademark, a proprietary name for a certain idea-factory, though the word was probably originated in 1919, by W. H. Smyth. Already the group has split into factions and disowned its spokesmen.

Fantastic claims have been made for the new system by more or less responsible persons, as they were made for such inventions or discoveries as the printing press, the telegraph, telephone, phonograph, moving picture, radio, Salvarsan, diphtheria serum, insulin, and whatnot.

Fantastic imposition, as always, arose at once. Ridicule and furious protest abound. The errors, or apparent errors, of the enthusiasts are held up to scorn; but as the world has both benefited and suffered from all other great inventions, so I think it will be with Technocracy.

The earliest announcements came up in the manner of Kipling's dawn, "like thunder." Press and public ran away with the idea. We had some over-hasty statements concerning the eminence of some of the sponsors. Mr. Howard Scott was the original wonder boy; he was credited with as many degrees as an nth-degree Mason.

Disemployment by technology mentioned above is on the lips of nearly everyone in North America today.)

Socialism and communism, by contrast, were outgrowths of an environment in which practically all work was done by human muscle power, and wherein it was never possible to produce sufficient goods and services for all citizens. Karl Marx's theories were formulated to overcome conditions as they existed in Europe in the middle of the nineteenth century—far different conditions from those faced in twentieth-century North America.

Only Technocracy applies the necessary measures to cope with twenty-first-century technological problems.

Did not Technocracy state in 1937 that the Price System would be over by 1942? If so, why do we still have it? What happened?

What happened is that we have had a world war and a series of smaller conflicts ever since. These have given massive blood transfusions to the ailing Price System and prolonged its life expectancy.

Furthermore, Technocracy did not make the bald, unqualified prediction stated above. Instead it indicated that if trends continued in the direction they were taking, the Price System would be in ever-increasing difficulty until it reached the point of breakdown. The mounting problems of the present system are plainly evident on every hand.

What can one do as an individual to bring about a better system?

We suggest that the best way to do this is to acquaint yourself as fully as possible on all aspects of the problem, after which an objective solution will commence to suggest itself. While anyone can do this individually and alone if one has the integrity and interest to do so, it seems rather a waste of time to go over ground that has already been covered with the likely result that a similar conclusion would be reached to one that has already been rather widely publicized.

We refer, of course, to Technocracy's social analysis and synthesis. Probably the best move individuals could make would be to join the organization of Technocracy Inc., investigate it from the inside, and prepare themselves in any way practical through the organization's media to inform other North Americans of Technocracy's conclusions.

If you feel that the organization does not have the answer, you can drop your membership more easily than you attained it.

What are the duties and obligations of members of Technocracy?

The only requirements for membership are to pay your dues ($15.00 a year) and to abide by the organization's bylaws and general regulations. Beyond that, your degree of participation depends upon your personal initiative.

Presuming, though, that you joined the organization because you were convinced that Technocracy holds the only answer to North America's social dilemma, you would wish to learn as much as possible as soon as possible about the organization. By so doing, you would be preparing yourself, through whatever personal knowledge or ability you may possess, to further Technocracy's objectives by informing your fellow North Americans about them.

The first step will be to attend a Study Class where, after either learning the rudiments of basic science or refreshing your memory of them, you will learn Technocracy's analysis of the existing society and why the Price System is incapable of solving its problems; the final lessons explain what is necessary for their solution.

Technocracy has room for many talents, such as teaching, speaking, writing, typing, accounting (since we are still in the Price System), printing, and a wide variety of others. The combination of these abilities through the efforts of its various members constitutes the full capability of Technocracy to inform North Americans of "the only organization that is preparing the people of this continent for social change." A member's most important obligation to Technocracy Inc. is one's sense of realization of that responsibility, coupled with a determination to carry it out.

What do Technocrats mean by social change? Their use of the term seems to differ from that of the popular understanding.

Very much so. Social change is far more basic than the periodic switches from one political party to another, even if these switches are from the far right to the far left; for unless the essential ingredient of social change is introduced by the new administration, nothing more than superficial differences will result.

The essential ingredient to effect social change is a change in the rate of energy conversion, whether this be upward or downward. Thus, a society that converts energy at a low rate can have only a low overall living standard, while another that converts energy at a higher rate can have a correspondingly higher standard of living for all its citizens. That this may not actually occur has nothing to do with society's ability to do so; the fault lies in the distributive mechanism.

For all practical purposes, we may consider social change to involve an upward adjustment of the ability to convert energy. Historically, from time immemorial until the last couple of centuries, the only significant means humankind had of converting energy was the power of their own muscles. This accounted for about 98 percent of all energy converted, notwithstanding the assistance obtained from such extraneous sources (those outside the human body) as domesticated animals, windmills, and waterfalls. Thus, the general living standard throughout the world in the middle of the eighteenth century was not substantially different from what it had been four or five thousand years earlier, which suggests that the rate of energy conversion was at its irreducible minimum.

The first significant change upward occurred when the energy of burning coal was harnessed for use through the medium of the newly invented steam engine in the eighteenth century. Slowly at first, but with rapidly gathering momentum, the trend to the use of extraneous sources of energy-coal, petroleum products, electricity-increased until today in North America an exact reverse of the historic situation exists. Less than 2 percent of all energy converted for the production of goods and services can be attributed to human muscle power; the balance, over 98 percent, comes from extraneous sources: technological energy, mechanical, electrical, or chemical. Accordingly, we now have the physical ability to produce an optimal amount of goods and services for every resident of the continent. The fact that they are not receiving it stems from their stubborn retention of that archaic Price System social mechanism that was conceived in natural scarcity and is operable only under those environmental conditions.

Membership in Technocracy Inc. includes a variety of responsibilities, none of which is more important than communicating to other people the significance of the scientific investigations of the Technical Alliance, the forerunner of Technocracy Incorporated.

What is your symbol called, and what is its significance? Would it, with the gray field, be the flag of the Technate?

The symbol is called the monad and it signifies balance between production and distribution, which is an integral part of the social program designed by Technocracy. Whether it and the gray field will be the flag of the Technate is a matter that will have to be determined by the citizens of the Technate.

Ferndale, WA
Technocracy Inc.
www.technocracyinc.com
Edmond D. Vongehr
54 1-661-5325

Concept and Organization

Questions in this section deal with the body of thought of Technocracy itself and with the organization formed to fill the need for disseminating that body of thought to all North Americans.

What is Technocracy?

Briefly, Technocracy is science applied to the social order. Science concerns itself with the determination of the most probable in any field of knowledge, be it chemistry, engineering, or social phenomena. Technocracy, then, concerns itself with the determination of the most probable in the field of social science-the determination of the most probable state of society. It has to do primarily with that part of the social mechanism relating to the production and distribution of goods and services, but it has many far-reaching implications.

How did Technocracy originate?

Technocracy had its inception in 1919 in New York City in an organization known as the Technical Alliance of North America. This group included in its ranks such people as Thorstein Veblen, a distinguished educator in the field of social science, sometimes called the "stormy petrel of American economics"; Charles Steinmetz of the General Electric Company, often referred to as "the wizard of

Schenectady"; consulting engineer and mathematician Bassett Jones; physics professor Richard Tolman; consulting architect Frederick L. Ackerman; and Stuart Chase, popular economist and author. Heading the group as chief engineer was Howard Scott, outstanding consulting and industrial engineer.

The primary aim of the Technical Alliance was to ascertain the possibility of applying the achievements of science to social and industrial affairs. With this in mind, they set about to make a survey of the energy and natural resources of the North American continent-all the territory included between the Panama Canal and the North Pole. In addition, they studied the industrial evolution that had taken place therein. They showed graphically the operating characteristics of the present industrial system with all its waste and leakage and worked out a tentative design of a completely coordinated system of production and distribution. Of course, they always kept in mind their aim, which was to provide a better standard of living for the people living on the continental area with the least possible waste of nonrenewable resources.

After nearly fourteen years of research, analysis, and synthesis, the Alliance's work, as such, was nearing completion when an enterprising newspaper reporter heard that something of more than usual interest was taking place at Columbia University. He spilled the story somewhat prematurely to his New York daily that gave it bannerline front-page coverage; and from there it spread rapidly across the continent, receiving front-page headlines in all major newspapers.

Unfortunately, much of the information contained in these newspaper stories was incorrect and misleading; so, it was apparent to the members of the Technical Alliance that the publicity measures they had planned for their findings would have to be implemented immediately rather than at the later date they had originally intended. These measures involved the disbandment of the purely research-oriented Technical Alliance and the formation of a new organization that would continue this important research and would also conduct a program of education to correctly inform North Americans of the findings and conclusions of the original group. The new organization would be called Technocracy Incorporated, the initial word being derived from Greek language roots to convey the overall concept of government by science. In the spring of 1933, the organization was incorporated under the laws of the State of New York as a nonsectarian, educational-research membership organization. The training of public speakers and the formation of study classes on a continental scale quickly followed.

What are the conclusions of Technocracy?

There are three basic conclusions. The first is that there exists on the North American continent a physical potential in resources to produce a high standard of goods and services for all citizens, and that the high-speed technology for converting these resources to use-forms in sufficient volume is already installed, and the skilled personnel for operating it are present and available. Yet we have unprecedented insecurity, extensive poverty, and rampant crime.

The second conclusion of Technocracy is that the Price System can no longer function adequately as a method of production and distribution of goods. The invention of power machinery has made it possible to produce a plethora of goods with a relatively small amount of human labor. As machines displace men and women, however, purchasing power is destroyed, for if people cannot work for wages and salaries, they cannot buy goods. We find ourselves, then, in this paradoxical situation: the more we produce, the less we are able to consume.

The final basic conclusion is that a new distributive system must be instituted that is designed to the special needs of an environment of technological adequacy, and that this system must not in any way be associated with the extent of an individual's functional contribution to society.

Could either Canada or the United States operate a Technate without the other?

No, because each nation in itself has deficiencies that in large measure can be met only by joining with the other. Canada, for instance, except for cereal grains, grows very little of its own food, depending otherwise mostly on importations from the climatically better located United States. On the other hand, Canada is far better endowed than the United States with certain essentials that the latter needs to sustain its technological mechanism. Important among these are fuel and energy resources, various metals, and abundant water supply, and accompanying hydroelectric power potential.

What are the social implications of Technocracy?

There are many. Take, for instance, the attainment of leisure. For the first time in history, people would be released from drudgery and their creative energies set free.

It would be impossible in a Technate to sue for breach of promise, alimony, breach of contract, damages, or to probate a will, because in a Technate all citizens would have a high, secure, individually chosen standard of living. As practically all crime in the Price System results from attempts of individuals to illegally acquire the property of others in order to alleviate their own insecurity, crime would practically cease to exist in a Technocratic Society.

In a Technate, citizens would be treated as human beings for the first time in their social history. They would no longer be considered mostly as a means of converting raw materials into usable products for the comfort and enhancement of a privileged few but would be freed by a provident technology to enjoy more of those products themselves along with the time to do so. In addition, they no longer would be subjected to the many legalistic prohibitions and monetary restraints that preclude participation in many desired pursuits, as is presently the case.

Is the Technocratic movement a political party?

No, it is not. Technocracy's sole reason for being is to promote its social program for institution when the Price System can no longer operate in North America. To run candidates for political office to advocate adoption of the program would quickly defeat the organization's whole purpose, for they would be unable to introduce any of the program's features on a local basis because of the continental scope of the program. Technocracy, by remaining entirely free from political entanglements, can promote its social program at the continental level without being restricted by the national or local boundaries of political limitations.

This is not to say that Technocracy will not consider political action in the future if the need arises, but such action would be only in a referendum calling for the acceptance or rejection of Technocracy's proposals. It is highly improbable that the program would be rejected in the face of badly deteriorated social circumstances that would likely prevail at the time of such referendum.

What would be done with the people whose present jobs, like banking, would cease to exist in a Technocracy society?

Many, of course, would be retired with full consuming privileges, having already passed the Technate retirement age of forty-five. The rest would be retrained for function in other roles, whatever their talents.

What are you going to do with the people who are not interested in Technocracy?

If the question asks what we intend to do with persons today who are not interested in Technocracy, the answer is "nothing." We are seeking people who are intelligent and open-minded enough to embrace a new idea. However, deteriorating economic and social conditions will force many people not presently interested to look in our direction.

In the Technate, even the people who are not interested in Technocracy will enjoy the same high standard of living and increased leisure along with greater opportunity for cultural activities. Should they still prefer to live somewhere else, there will be no restriction on emigration.

Is not Technocracy very similar to socialism or communism?

No, it is not-mainly because it proceeds from entirely different premises than either socialism or communism. Technocracy originated out of a circumstance of technologically produced disemployment. Research indicated that increasing technological-disemployment would render impossible the distribution of sufficient consuming power in salaries and wages to buy back the products of increasingly efficient machines. The social program of Technocracy, therefore, is one specifically designed to distribute an optimum of goods and services to all citizens.

Greater technological efficiency is needed, but we really won't stop the overconsumption of the world's resources without some very serious political and economic change. This planet is round, but if we don't wake up from the dream of growth we'll sleepwalk right over the edge.

Stan Cox is a member of the Prairie Writers Circle and senior research scientist at the Land Institute, a natural systems agriculture research organization in Salina, Kansas. He holds a doctorate in plant breeding from Iowa State University.

Published on Friday, June 6, 2003, by CommonDreams.org

Tax Cuts while Problems
of Homeless Grow

By Ralph Nader

Two views of the nation's capital were on display last week.

At 1600 Pennsylvania Avenue, the main event was the ceremony for President Bush's signing of still another massive tax cut designed primarily for the wealthy. On hand were the usual bevy of reporters and cameras to record the event. There were Republican leaders from the House and Senate full of self-praise for their legislative achievement that will balloon the deficit and drain funding from critical federal programs.

A dozen blocks away, some five hundred health workers from all over the country were gathered in a hotel ballroom to discuss ways to meet the desperate need for housing and health care for the nation's growing population of homeless Americans. None of the Republican leadership brass was in sight and no media showed to carry forth the message of the desperate plight of people without shelter or health care or hope.

High on the agenda of the advocates for the homeless—whose organization is formally known as Health Care for the Homeless (HCH)-is the closing of the enormous gap in the supply of affordable housing. The nation is five to six million units short of the demand for the barest affordable housing. This fact places heavy pressure on the effort to find decent shelter for low-and moderate-income families.

Fourteen million families spend more than half of their entire income on housing, much of it crowded and substandard, leaving little for other necessities such as food, clothing, and medical care.

The Department of Housing and Urban Development has long urged that families try to keep their housing outlays to less than 30 percent of their income. Any payout for housing beyond that often leads to serious economic problems which push families into bankruptcy and homelessness—not to mention the fact that many forgo proper nutrition and medical care in an attempt to keep their homes.

Meanwhile at Bush's White House tax-cut ceremony, it was obvious that the political oligarchies were not thinking about affordable housing or, for that matter, any other pressing economic need of the nation. Needs? What needs? It's party time for the wealthy as the Treasury is emptied for them.

This means that critically important social and economic programs will be put off for years while the nation struggles out of budget deficits created by the 2001 and 2003 tax cuts and the rising costs of the invasion and prolonged occupation of Iraq. This will have a serious negative impact on the national economy in coming years. Future administrations and future generations will have to struggle with the consequences long after George W. Bush has left office and is lounging under a mesquite tree in Crawford, Texas.

But, the impact on homeless people and families is immediate. Not only will affordable housing programs be pushed to the background, but the other big need of the homeless—adequate universal health care—will slide further down the national agenda if the budget deficits balloon.

Homelessness is increasing and along with it a growing number of serious health problems, some contagious. It is difficult to pin down the exact number of homeless at a given moment, but a 2001 study by Helping America's Homeless estimated that 842,000 people were homeless in a given week and 3.5 million became homeless over the course of a year. A 1995 study reports that over a five-year period 2 to 3 percent of the US population will experience at least one night of homelessness.

Many of the homeless are the working poor who earn only the minimum wage of $5.15 an hour—totally inadequate in today's housing market. The purchasing power of the minimum wage is less than a third of the minimum wage of 1968. How can minimum-wage families exist—even put proper food on the table and clothe their children, much less pay rent in today's market? A worker would have to earn $14.66 an hour to provide enough income to afford a two-bedroom home at the national weighted Fair Market Rent (FMR). With the unemployment rate at 6 percent and rising, the problem of homelessness is only going to worsen.

A survey by the US Conference of Mayors found that requests for emergency shelter increased an average of 19 percent in major cities last year. In many cities—often having subsidized gleaming stadiums with tax dollars—the requests had to be rejected because the cities lacked sufficient beds. Lack of a stable place to live is traumatic for adults, but for children the experience is particularly cruel. More than 1.35 million children are homeless at some point each year. They exist in shelters, cars, parks or pushed into already badly overcrowded quarters. The homeless life disrupts their education, exposes them to communicable diseases, malnutrition, depression, and drug addictions.

It is difficult to imagine a worse environment for a child or young adult. What kind of nation do we have when we allow children to be dropped through the safety nets and left on the streets or in crowded shelters? Of course many of the safety nets have been shredded through welfare reform efforts, benefit retractions, and the declining value of the frozen minimum wage. The growing income gap between the poorest and wealthiest citizens have left an increasing number of families at risk of homelessness, including those with young children.

We can solve the problem of poverty and homelessness. But it will take more than the "Alice in Wonderland" economics of the Bush Administration which believes there is only one solution to all problems-cut taxes for the wealthy who, unlike working families, do not spend their Bush bonus.

We need to get off this plutocratic tax-cutting binge and start grappling with real solutions to real problems. Liberals and progressives are willing to share with the majority; conservatives and right-wingers hoard everything for themselves, the minority.

Comment:

The only hope of relief to the steadily increasing level of poverty is to place purchasing power into the affected citizens' pockets. The pattern of reducing employees and or relocating business overseas will only worsen the condition. This article by Mr. Nader is informative, but it does nothing to suggest a solution, and that is because in our present economic and social structure there can be no solution. Wake up, people. Investigate Technocracy to visualize a grand new way to live.

Editor
www.technocracyinc.org

An Explanation

In presenting a magazine to the public that represents the concepts of Technocracy Inc., we must be judicious in using the limited space that printing a quarterly periodical allows. We have to opt out in describing most of the political machinations of late pertaining to the Bush administration and we do so for several reasons. The main reason is that only by degree are they any different than in the past, and another reason is that although it feels good to get back at them in some way, we still cannot do anything about it. We do however feel obligated to highlight the most egregious examples especially ones showing great social and environmental harm.

As members of Technocracy we must realize that it is inevitable that our society go through something akin to what is now happening. Our job is not to emphasize the political battles pitting one dangerously outdated concept against another, but to show the consequences of not recognizing that those actions have no chance of doing anything but to make our precarious situation much worse. The Price System is in sharp decline in its ability to function. We should thank Bush and company for accelerating the process, not joining in the complete uselessness of some kind of political remedy.

It was explained to me years ago from the writings of Howard Scott and other early Technocrats, that what we are beginning to experience will be of the most dangerous and critical time. We have to keep our eye our goal-the opportunity to explain and educate that there is only one way out and that is by implementing scientific functional governance, and not be distracted by offers to "fix" the situation within the same system that must be discarded if we are to survive.

Good luck to all of us.

George Wright
Editor
The North American Technocrat

Our Economy

Miracle Grow!

Published on Friday, May 16, 2003, by CommonDreams.org by Stan Cox

Prairie Writers Circle

"Dream" is the key word. Our economic system is grounded in the fantasy that consumption can grow forever and without limit, both in North America and throughout the planet.

The way the House and Senate have been battling over tax cuts and other money matters lately, you'd think some sweeping economic changes had been proposed. But when a debate becomes this boisterous, it's actually a sure sign that everyone is in full agreement on the fundamental issues.

Suppose the following resolution were introduced in Congress: "Resolved: Economic growth is good." It would pass both chambers without a single nay. An amendment stating, "And faster growth is better," would probably pass on an easy voice vote.

Politicians like growth because the problems of society appear to shrink in an expanding economy. For one thing, growth provides an excuse to ignore this country's widening rich-poor gap. Inequality. org, a monitoring website, reports that the richest 5 percent of families own 60 percent of the wealth, while the average net worth of Americans in the bottom 40 percent is just about zero.

Redistribution of that wealth is not discussed in polite company. So when Washington politicians or Wall Street economists offer lower-income Americans their usual little sliver of the economic pie, they have to conjure up a dream of an ever-expanding pie offering bigger slices for everyone, sometime in the future.

"Dream" is the key word. Our economic system is grounded in the fantasy that consumption can grow forever and without limit, both in America and throughout the planet.

In his Earth Day statement in April, President Bush pretended otherwise: "We will promote energy efficiency and security, and improve and protect water quality, while encouraging economic growth." But that's a list of goals that clash, inevitably and often. When they do, Bush, as do most all politicians, opted for growth.

We have already carried this fantasy too far. Oakland-based Redefining Progress (www.rprogress.org) recently evaluated the ecological effect of people living in 146 nations. The organization estimated the average consumption per person in each country and compared it with the ability of that country's territory to provide the resources and handle the wastes.

In the United States, we consume and discard at a rate that exceeds our country's biological carrying capacity by 83 percent. We import resources from other countries to make this possible. So does the rest of the industrialized world: the populations of the 10 richest countries, including the US, overshoot their carrying capacity by an average of 85 percent.

These numbers represent a much more troubling deficit than the merely fiscal shortfalls that now plague our federal and state governments. We gobble resources and throw off wastes at almost twice the rate that can be supported by our land mass and biological systems. Redefining Progress's estimates are conservative; they do not include some hard-to-quantify damage like loss of biodiversity.

The World Bank reported in April that rich countries, with 15 percent of the world's population, account for half of all energy consumption and carbon dioxide emissions. The Organization for Economic Cooperation and Development says that because of economic growth in thirty advanced capitalist nations, their municipal waste output increased 40 percent—almost twice as fast as population growth-from 1980 to 2000.

Don't we just need more resource-efficient growth? We already have it, in some areas of the economy. The Rocky Mountain Institute in Colorado reports that by the year 2000, the US economy used 39 percent less energy to generate a dollar's worth of growth than it did in 1975. But that impressive savings has been almost entirely eaten up by headlong growth of the economy. Energy use—overall and per person—has risen steadily for the past twenty years. The typical American now consumes 6 percent more energy than in 1983.

Suppose a technology were developed that cut resource use in half. In the irresistible logic of capitalism, that would be a signal to double production, not to exercise restraint. Even if business were slow, we'd be much more likely to see "buy one, get one free" specials than "50 percent off" sales.

Comment:

If price system economics has long recognized this free ride, why haven't they solved the vast waste of resources?

Do You Know?

We, as a society, face many problems as a result of operating in a Price System: poverty, unemployment, inadequate education, ditto for our health system, a crumbling infrastructure, and a huge monetary deficit, both individually, and at all levels of government. It should be obvious that our present form of social administration is unable to function efficiently in a technological society. However, the plight of our monetary system is but nothing, compared to what we are doing to the physical world we live in, this planet we depend on for our very existence.

There are three things essential to life; air, water, and nourishment. Another consideration for mammals is a degree of warmth. Life in all its essential forms must have these things in order to exist. While water is plentiful, 70 percent of the planet is covered by water, of this amount 97 percent is seawater and is undrinkable. Therefore, only 3 percent is classified as fresh, and 75 percent of this is locked solid in the Earth's glaciers and polar ice caps. Another 14 percent of that 3 percent is underground water that is too deep to tap. A miniscule 0.027 percent of the fresh water flows in rivers and lies in aquifers. Some aquifers are recharged by rain, but some, because of their depth, are not being recharged. Much of the small amount of fresh water available is polluted by chemicals drifting through the air, by chemicals and leakage from toxic dumps, from fertilizer runoff, from raw sewage, salt, and erosion. The Ogallala Aquifer, the largest underground reservoir in the world, runs under six states. However, there are now two hundred thousand wells pumping water from this aquifer. Some experts predict it will be gone in forty years, then what? Today it irrigates most of the Midwest and allows huge quantities of grain to be grown.

Another essential to life, air which is badly polluted in many parts of North America; sulfur emissions, nitrous oxides, and hydrocarbons are just a few. Many pollutants also change chemically; rain, for example, combined with smoke stack emissions, produces sulfuric acid, which settles on the ground and into waterways, impairing our ability to grow food, poisoning water, killing aquatic life and trees. About twenty-five billion tons of topsoil disappears every year. That topsoil is needed to grow food, to feed an ever-expanding number of people from a declining soil base and water base. There are increasing problems of climatic modification caused by increasing use of fossil fuels, leading to a buildup of carbon dioxide, coupled with mounting evidence of a breakdown in the ozone layer surrounding this planet.

We are consuming or destroying 40 percent of the total output of photosynthesis that is the source of all nutrition. Half of the rainforest in tropical areas have already been lost; an area the size of Kansas is being lost every year to clear cutting for timber, cattle grazing, housing, and fuel. We are witnessing the destruction of the environment as people search for food and fuel. Realize that these serious and mounting assaults on our planet are being caused by our present population of a little over six billion. This number is expected to double in the next thirty years (it could also decline very rapidly). The depredations now being wrought on this planet will be aggravated that much more as long as the population continues to increase. This is the only planet we can exist on; we exist or perish right here. Whether we can survive as a species depends on how we treat the environment. Our present actions do not bode well for our future well-being. We must conserve water, remove pollutants, stop our massive destruction of forests, curb the buildup of carbon dioxide, reduce drastically the use of many chemicals, reduce soil erosion, and build an atmosphere in the world where cooperation is possible so that most of these problems can be addressed. In a world governed by money, given to short-term economic expediency, and political and business considerations, such cooperation is impossible. More of these abuses will occur; therefore, our future is bleak indeed.

The world is in the grip of opposing ideologies, none of them have any ideas concerning governance without money and politics and none of them with any design of governance for the future. Some want to cling to the concept of the good old days, which if they ever existed, did so only for a few. There are the egalitarians, attempting to share out the misery, bringing all down to the lowest common denominator. They seek equality, which is unobtainable in any social system. We still engage in tribal warfare to settle our differences. War has always been a means of taking people's minds off of their real problems, their real source of misery. Leaders provoke wars, some incident, real or imagined is staged with some other country, and then they all bravely march off to war, prepared to lay down their lives for something that they never really had in the first place.

Social change is inevitable. Whether it will be beneficial remains to be seen. The only constant is change; to attempt to maintain the status quo is in effect flogging a dead horse. As engineers and technologists design equipment to operate at higher speeds, with greater energy consumption per unit of time, and using less energy per unit produced of products or services, they are bringing about those very things that will force social change. Intelligence is defined as the ability to adapt to changing circumstances or environment. On the basis of that definition, we show very little or none. Are you aware of what is happening in society today and, more to the point, why? Have you considered the long-term effects of action being taken today? If so, you should show some interest in what is occurring and take some action to ensure a worthwhile future.

For survival, we must operate on the basis of function, allowing the methods of science to deal with the problems now besetting us, and allowing the methods of science to cope with these problems of technology being misused and abused. We must deal with problems that affect this planet and those that live on it. We must find solutions that will benefit all of its inhabitants and secure the chance of longtime survival for all. Technocracy has such a program, well researched and designed for application on the North American continent, its principle applicable anywhere. We have passed the time of choice. Technocracy's program is mandatory if we are to survive. Investigate the concept; think about the ramifications of what we are now doing and the bleak future facing us, then act accordingly.

—John Darvill
Member of Technocracy Inc.

The Damned

Reprinted from *The Technocrat*
December 1977

Economic depression is a way of life for millions of North Americans, including the poor, the afflicted (mentally as well as physically), the incarcerated, and the addicted.

The poor generally live in bad housing in slums and in racial and ethnic ghettos. Diet is in adequate and clothing is not substantial. They are usually short changed when it comes to education and health protection. Recreational outlets are a real luxury.

If you are poor and physically sick, you are doubly damned. You will not receive the immediate attention of a physician, but instead, wait endless hours in the line at the free clinic. If you are seriously ill but not poor, the exorbitant cost of medical and hos pit al care will soon threaten, if not deplete, your financial resources.

If you have mental problems of a serious nature, whether congenital or of later development, no matter what your economic stat us, life will not be a bowl of cherries. If you have to be institutionalized, you may wind up in one of what have been referred to in recent scandals as "warehouses for people."

Prisons are well known as breeders of crime. Gestures toward re habilitation are just that, gestures. Recidivism is rampant. The "outside" to an ex-convict is not exactly congenial.

People who are addicted to alcohol or other drugs mostly find life a living hell. Often they are where they are because they cannot cope with a hostile environment. Addiction to hard drugs is an expensive habit and almost inevitably leads to crime to try and support it.

All this is in the wealthiest area in the world!

However, for all their numbers, there are not enough of these second-and third-class citizens to make their plight socially intolerable. So we plod along.

At present, the United States and Canada are experiencing a general slump. Some call it recession, some call it depression. Whatever.

If the slump eases so that even a few of the damned will be helped, good for them. If the slump stabilizes so that the status quo remains as it is, that will have to do. A relatively few voices in the wilderness are not going to make that much difference.

But if the crisis deepens, as it will if the analysis of Technocracy proves correct, then the synthesis of Technocracy, its social program, will be an idea to be reckoned with by an ever-increasing number of people.

Editorial

Yes, this continent is at the brink of extinction. And, on our cover, we asked the question: Now, will you listen to us?

Over sixty-five years ago, Technocracy started by advising the public what would happen if the financiers and politicians were allowed to misuse the great technology that was advancing so rapidly. Well, the misuse of technology was allowed, and it also started advancing rapidly; but as the misuse continued to this day, Technocracy has never stopped explaining the scientific and logical reasons why, and how, this misuse must be stopped. Obviously, the propaganda of the politicians and their financial backers, whipping up gallons of hocus-pocus, was easier for the public to swallow. It was easier for them to not have to do any thinking, nor put any effort to make any real changes in their social system. They considered it to be risky. Just the act of dropping the Price System would have done it; no money would mean no politicians and no financiers to mess things up the way they are doing.

Now, Technocracy just didn't evolve out of nothing. Some of the greatest minds in the world, each one in their fields of expertise, made a scientific study of every physical sequence of the whole continent, and fitted them all together to see how each physical change would affect the rest of the sequences. To take one example, if contamination of a river was not allowed in one province or state, but allowed to happen in the next province or state, then those first efforts to keep it clean would have been useless. The physical means of the whole continent have to be coordinated so that these contaminations wouldn't take place. Piecemeal doesn't do it!

Technocracy used science, which showed how one phase must interact with another to provide the clean water, clean soil, clean food, and clean air needed for all the citizens of the continent. All their findings showed that their scientific reasoning was synchronized with nature.

They then began to publish their findings so that they could pass on this Technological Social Design to the public as a plan to follow to correct the mistakes made by misusing technology.

The most important change to be made, (and this was shown by scientific study) was that money (the Price System), and the political system, had to be abolished in order for the Technological Design to work. It was the scientists' concern over productive capacity at that time—why more was being produced with less man-hours of labor—which was the reason for the research in the first place. "To work" meant it had to benefit the citizens of the continent. The benefits accrued to people would be a byproduct of the design.

Now, "that time" has passed into "this time," which is now treating people of the continent so that, soon, they will not even survive.

The one thing that Technocracy could not do was to get people to think scientifically, to be able to see the damage the misuse of technology was causing. Technocracy could not make people understand that they must discard the political and financial social system which controlled the technology on the continent. Technocrats could not make the changes that were needed; they could only advise and try to educate the public that scientific methods would work by using technology properly, in order to benefit all of the citizens. So, it had to be the citizens themselves who, en masse, would have to instigate, and demand, that the necessary changes be put in motion—the necessary changes in their social system—before it collapsed entirely. Well, collapse is nearly here. And no new social system has been installed.

If you don't, even now, think our continent is in trouble, read our list of the many things which are destroying our quality of life. Check through each one. There is, probably, not one that you, yourself, don't know about. Most certainly, every one of them has been highlighted in a news item at some time. Some of them may go so far as to destroy not only our quality of life, but life itself.

All is not lost, however, as, even now, although some resources are gone forever, it is still not too late to make a change in the social system—a complete change—and that means discarding the monetary system (or Price System, as we call it).

Properly trained technicians in charge of our technology would bring the proper use of technology. And, in every industry, in medicine, in health care, in education, in the arts, in ecology, where these functions are led by properly trained people in their fields, vast beneficial changes would be made. Just think of your own lives—how they would be affected without money being a deterrent.

If people themselves don't change the present social system, we will all see some terrible changes made for us, just because of plain stupidity.

So, now, will you listen to us?

—Editor

Apathy

Technocracy's social program is the natural synthesis of the application of the scientific method to a particular social problem—that of determining how to keep the physical equipment of North America operating when the Price System control ceases to operate. This was the prime consideration, for roughly 90 percent of North Americans are completely dependent upon the continuous operation of their technological equipment for their very survival. Without the uninterrupted operation of that equipment, we not only would not have abundance; we would not have our lives.

Technocracy is an educational research organization. It is not here for any other purpose than to attempt to inform the people of North America of the nature of the problems which now confront us, and what can be done to alleviate these problems to bring about a society more in keeping with the age in which we live. Technocracy is not responsible for the problems we have, today. Technocracy can do little or nothing about them, except talk to people to try to make them understand what is happening. And these people will have to join together to demand that the changes suggested by Technocracy be instituted.

If Technocracy disappeared tomorrow, the problems that we talk about will still exist, and they will still continue to degrade our society. Nothing will change until people think in terms of function, and not in terms of "the bottom line"—money.

—Cyril Large
158 Promenade Dr., No. 303 Nanaimo, BC V9R 6M7

Technocracy Inc.

A Chance, Not a Choice
Information Brief Number 54

Too often a person investigating Technocracy for the first time assumes that he is being confronted with a social idea which he may choose to accept or reject on the basis of how well it pleases him—as though he were being asked to switch from one brand of merchandise to another brand purportedly a little better than the one he already uses. He feels that he has a choice as to the kind of social system he shall live in, and he tends to evaluate Technocracy on how well it appeals to his subjective desires.

As in the case of most assumptions, this one is in error. Technocracy is not being "sold" in competition with other alternatives. When one attempts to sell an idea, it implies that he seeks to benefit from that sale, that there is something in it for him. So, a second erroneous assumption is the one that Technocrats are promulgating their program in the hope that they will someday take over the society and rule it according to their Technocratic blueprint. These assumptions evidently arise from along term of conditioning in the vagaries of politics.

Technocracy is presented on the basis that it is a carefully engineered design for operating the social system of North America, either when the prevailing programs prove unable to function or when enough social enlightenment develops among the citizens to install it. Technocrats serve in the role of designers and advisers. Their purpose is to facilitate the change when the time comes. But they do not seek to take over or to operate the technological social design they specify for this continent. Individual members of Technocracy have a wide range of subjective reasons for being active in the organization. Some may favor a switch from the Price System to Technocracy because they have an abhorrence of the profligate waste and extreme corruption that are characteristic features of Price System operations. Some may be motivated by a desire for a higher standard of living for themselves along with the greater security that would result from applying science to society. Or one may join Technocracy for no better reason than to spite a neighbor or a relative who is a staunch disciple of Free Enterprise and Rugged Individualism. These subjective reasons of the members are important to the individual members, but as every Technocrat knows, what really counts is the strategic analysis and the social design that will give citizens of North America the means to achieve survival.

Technocracy has analyzed the physical changes occurring on this continent and has plotted their future course, not from the standpoint of personal desires but in accordance with the direction in which events are headed. Technocrats are fully aware that irreversible changes are taking place. They know that the future of North American society is not being decided by the whims, desires, and hopes of individuals, but by the force of events. They know that the old order of scarcity, toil and insecurity is coming to an end. They know that the next stage will be either chaos, with widespread man-made destruction, out of which will emerge a low order of fascism (if, indeed any human life survives) or a new order based on an intelligent stewardship of physical things and a vastly more efficient operation of our technological society.

The developing trends are not a matter which individuals can decide for themselves or prevent. All they can do is take one of four general courses: (1) help facilitate the change to a new social order, making the change more orderly and peaceful; (2) fight against this change, fostering violence and destruction; (3) remain indifferent to events around them; or (4) dissipate themselves in minor controversies, letting major trends develop without their willful participation. In any event, North Americans cannot escape the consequences of the developing trends.

The only practical and sensible decision of the individual is that of adapting to change, not fighting it or ignoring it. Technocracy is not creating change or even the course of change; rather, it is preparing for the next most probable state of society on the North American continent. That state of society is being "dictated" by the rate at which energy is being converted and by the machines that it powers.

Science and technology are, by nature, progressive (as contrasted to politics, economics, and theology which, by nature, are stagnant). Science and technology cannot be suppressed without endangering the survival of the human species, and there are certain reactionaries who despise progress so much that they would rather see mankind destroyed than see social change.

Within the scarcity conditions of the Price System, there may be a choice between communism and fascism, between liberalism and conservatism; but, in an area of high-energy technological production there is only one "choice"-functional control. Technology cannot be operated by opinion or desire, only by know-how and skill; but, by contrast, your act of voting in a political system will assure you of one thing: you will be having an incompetent managing the affairs of your country—a politician!

Goods and services, when they are sufficient to provide an adequate standard of living for all, cannot be dispensed by means of exchange values, only by giving them away, and even that has its limits. People cannot use more than they need, even as a gift. A system of measurement of consumption is essential to an efficient operation of an economy—to prevent overproduction and waste.

When the work of an area is done by wholly automatic machines (or by those requiring a minimum of human attention), the idea of one's earning a living through a job of work becomes ridiculous. When all citizens are guaranteed equal access to all the goods and services they can consume, there can be no masters and servants. A whole new social concept is required to fit the conditions that are developing on this continent.

So, the problem facing the individual citizen of North America is not one of choosing among various social alternatives for the future. In the long run, it has to be a functional operation—or else. Therefore, Technocracy cannot offer a choice as to how the society shall be operated, but Technocracy's design does offer a chance for North American citizens such as mankind has never been offered before—a chance to have the best quality of life that an energy- and resource-efficient technological society can provide.

May you, as a citizen of this continent, make the most of it.

www.technocracyinc.org

For further information about Technocracy and membership requirements, contact Technocracy Inc. (www.technocraryinc.org).

Technocracy

Technocracy originated in the winter of 1918–1919 when Howard Scott formed a group of scientists, engineers, and economists that became known in 1920 as the Technical Alliance—a research organization. In 1933, it was incorporated under the laws of the State of New York as a nonprofit, nonpolitical, nonsectarian membership organization. It has no affiliation with any other organization, group, or association either in North America or elsewhere.

Technocracy was built in North America by North Americans. It is composed of North American citizens of all walks of life. Technocracy's membership is a composite of all the occupations, economic levels, races, and religions that make up this continent. Membership is open only to North American citizens.

Technology Does Replace Man-Hours

No political method, in Washington, Ottawa, or elsewhere is going to fix this economy. Why? Because it can't be fixed. In the US, every president since, and including F. D. Roosevelt (when campaigning for office) has promised to balance the budget. Every one of them has failed to do so. Why? Because something they haven't considered has interfered with every attempt. The technological progression in this country and on this continent has rendered this economic system obsolete. It is so out of sync with this high-energy civilization that its complete collapse is imminent. It requires an ever-increasing growth of debt to further postpone the necessity of replacing this system with one specifically designed for this high-speed, highly technical, high-energy social system. And this process has driven the debt so high that it has about reached the limit that will still barely allow money to retain its value.

The federal debt has quadrupled in the past twelve years to $4 trillion. The total national debt, including the federal debt, is $15 trillion and is increasing at about $1 trillion per year. The interest alone at 8 percent on all this debt is about $4,800 per capita. And this amount is increasing at the rate of $320 each year for each individual, on average. A family of four is now paying about $19,200 per year. And it's increasing. How long can this continue? This is what Americans are now paying to maintain the operation of this obsolete economic system.

This economic system is so antiquated that it allows 35.7 million Americans to live in poverty, and this is just another cost of maintaining the system. This economic system of price, based on a system of scarcity values, has been obsolete since 1929, and has been kept alive by increasing the debt. An alternate method was designed and has been available since 1933. At that time, hundreds of articles were published in the press, but then the lid was clamped tight. The conspiracy of silence concerning this alternative method has been quite effective in withholding this information from the citizens of the US and Canada. Since a considerable amount of time is required for the general public to absorb the complex technicalities of such a change (it could require years), a continuation of this silence can only be construed as an act of treason against the people of this continent.

Who ever heard of anyone who had worked, or clawed, his way to the top in any type of social system being willing to change the system in which he was so successful? Those people are the status quo, the chief upholders of the existing system. And why shouldn't they be? The system has been good to them. However, in the US and Canada those people are finding it increasingly difficult to keep the increasing numbers of the distressed, poverty-stricken, homeless citizens believing in the methods which have worked so well for the rich.

The time has come when the political leaders of North America must produce results or get off the pot.

— The Los Angeles riots prove that
— Increasing crime proves it
— Increasing poverty, homelessness, and the underinsured prove it
— The present environmental degradation proves it
— The breakdown of school financing proves it
— Increasing industrial unemployment proves it

And, most of all, the total combination of all the above, plus much more altogether, proves it beyond any doubt!

The increase, for the first time in years, in the number of Americans voting may be a last desperate effort to solve, by existing rules, the economic problems of this country.

The citizens of this continent have also been misinformed about the advantages that could be available as a result of the technological progression. The technology now existing, if operated efficiently, could provide every North American with the highest living standard ever known by mankind. Poverty could, for the first time in history, be eliminated from an entire continent. Man-hours of human labor could be decreased significantly, and one's income would no longer be determined by the number of hours he worked.

All those physical requirements are now available for North America to produce plenty for every citizen. All that is required is for the citizens of this continent to wake up. We destroy the potatoes and pay farmers to produce less; we ship everything possible abroad in exchange for money, and we do it because we can produce more than we can sell for a price and a profit in our own country. It's this system of debt and scarcity that doesn't allow our own people to be cared for first.

The present economic system is in a process of collapse as a result of being unable (too inefficient) to cope with the increasing demands of a technological society. When it is replaced with an intelligent method, North Americans will, for the first time in human history, be able to enjoy freedom from economic restrictions. Isn't that worth investigating? Then investigate Technocracy.

—L. W. Nicholson
www.technocratinc.org

Declaration of Independence from Corporate Rule

We the People, in order to make Democracy real and justice possible, to defend against oppression, fight for the welfare of all and to liberate our minds and hearts, and to free our pocketbooks from the clutches of corporations and the wealthy, do hereby declare our Independence from Corporate Rule, shouting for all to hear that:

- Corporations are not persons and have no inherent inalienable human rights under the Constitution.
- Money is not speech. Money is concentrated capital and it cannot speak.
- Communities have the right to protect our land, our environment, our homes, our health, and all of our citizens-children, elders, workers, the sick and the poor-against actions to overturn democratically enacted laws. Corporations cannot use our democratically enacted laws against us.

The Supreme Court has decided the opposite, ruling that corporations have inalienable human rights, that money is speech, and that spending money to "speak" is protected under the First Amendment, and that corporations can overturn democratically enacted laws that protect elections, our safety and health, the environment, and the right to organize.

This shall not stand! We the People will overrule the Court!

And so, to protect our democracy, our health, our lives, our families, our communities, and our futures, we move to amend the United States Constitution to affirm that only real people-human beings-are sovereign and entitled to inalienable human rights protected under the Constitution.

www.MoveToAmend.org

Move to Amend

End Corporate Rule
Legalize Democracy

What Could Change if Corporate Personhood Were Abolished?

If We the People are sovereign, we must control the government. Corporations are created and chartered by the government which, acting on behalf of We the People, gives corporations privileges, not rights. Neither the government, without the consent of the governed, nor corporations have the right to rule over the people. Since corporations have gained the legal status of persons, corporations have accumulated rights and become rulers—in other words, they can tell the government what to do.

Corporate legal personhood was wrongly given—not by We the People, but by nine Supreme Court judges in 1886. Corporate personhood is bad for democracy, people, and the planet because it has allowed an artificial entity to legally relegate people to subhuman status. We the People have the sovereign right—indeed, duty—to abolish corporate personhood.

When corporate personhood is abolished, here are some actions We the People can take that are currently "beyond our authority":

1. Prohibit all political activity by corporations—stop all corporate political donations and all corporate lobbying.

These activities are currently legal because "corporate per-sons" are protected under the First Amendment.

2. Prevent corporate mergers and prohibit corporations from owning stock in other corporations. Regulation of these activities was overturned because "corporate persons" are protected under the due process clause of the Fourteenth Amendment.

3. Inspect for environmental or health violations without a warrant or prior notice. The Fourth Amendment protects "corporate persons" from search without a warrant, pro-tecting corporate polluters from concerned citizens and regulatory agencies.

4. Revoke corporate charters by popular referendum. This is now illegal because "corporate persons" are entitled to equal protection and due process under the Fourteenth Amendment.

5. Prohibit the erection of cell phone towers and chain stores from doing business in your town, county, and state. Civil rights legislation and the Fourteenth Amendment are used to ensure that "corporate persons" have an equal opportu-nity to be part of our communities.

6. Stop advertising for tobacco, guns, and other dangerous products. "Corporate persons" are entitled to free speech under the First Amendment, with "commercial speech" increasingly protected by the federal courts.

7. Levy differential taxes for corporations and restrict their size. The Fourteenth Amendment protects "corporate persons" from unfair discrimination (although they don't complain when they get big tax breaks).

8. Require labeling of genetically modified foods. This is cur-rently prevented because the First Amendment protects the right of "corporate persons" not to speak.

If corporate personhood were abolished, none of these things would change automatically. New laws could be written and old laws could be challenged in court to eliminate the kinds of protections that have enabled "corporate persons" to amass so much wealth and power.

Remember: judge-made law is not democracy! We the People have the power to change this.

This list was compiled by the Womens International League for Peace and Freedom, a coalition partner with MoveToAmend.org.

End Corporate Rule • Legalize Democracy • MoveToAmend.org
(707) 269-0984

A Contract for the American Dream

"I have a dream. It is a dream deeply rooted in
the American Dream" (Rev. Dr. Martin Luther
King Jr., March 1963, Washington).

We, the American people, promise to defend and advance a simple
ideal: liberty and justice for all. Americans who are willing to
work hard and play by the rules should be able to find a decent job,
get a good home in a strong community, retire with dignity, and give
their kids a better life. Every one of us—rich, poor, or in between,
regardless of skin color or birthplace, no matter their sexual orien-
tation or gender—has the right to life, liberty, and the pursuit of
happiness. That is our covenant, our compact, our contract with one
another. It is a promise we can fulfill but only by working together.

Today, the American dream is under threat. Our veterans are
coming home to few jobs and little hope on the home front. Our
young people are graduating off a cliff, burdened by heavy debt, into
the worst job market in half a century. The big banks that American
taxpayers bailed out won't cut homeowners a break. Our firefighters,
nurses, cops, and teachers—America's everyday heroes—are being
thrown out onto the street. We believe the following:

America is not broke. America is rich—still the wealthiest nation
ever. But too many at the top are grabbing the gains. No person or
corporation should be allowed to take from America while giving
little or nothing back. The superrich who got tax breaks and bailouts

should now pay full taxes and help create jobs here, not overseas. Those who do well in America should do well by America.

Americans need jobs, not cuts. Many of our best workers are sitting idle, while the work of rebuilding America goes undone. Together, we must rebuild our country, reinvest in our people, and jump-start the industries of the future. Millions of jobless Americans would love the opportunity to become working, tax-paying members of their communities again. We have a jobs crisis, not a deficit crisis.

To produce this contract for the American dream, 131,203 Americans came together online and in their communities. We wrote and rated 25,904 ideas. Together, we identified the ten most critical steps to get our economy back on track and restore the American dream:

★ 1. Invest in America's infrastructure.
Rebuild our crumbling bridges, dams, levees, ports, water and sewer lines, railways, roads, and public transit. We must invest in high-speed internet and a modem, energy-saving electric grid. These investments will create good jobs and rebuild America. To help finance these projects, we need national and state infrastructure banks.

★ 2. Create twenty-first-century energy jobs.
We should invest in American businesses that can power our country with innovative technologies like wind turbines, solar panels, geothermal systems, hybrid and electric cars, and next-generation batteries. And we should put Americans to work making our homes and buildings energy efficient. We can create good, green jobs in America, address the climate crisis, and build the clean energy economy.

★ 3. Invest in public education.
We should provide universal access to early childhood education, make school funding equitable, invest in high-quality teachers, and build safe, well-equipped school buildings

for our students. A high-quality education system, from universal preschool to vocational training and affordable higher education, is critical for our future and can create badly needed jobs now.

★ 4. Offer Medicare for all.
We should expand Medicare so it's available to all Americans and reform it to provide even more cost-effective, quality care. The Affordable Care Act is a good start and we must implement it, but it's not enough. We can save trillions of dollars by joining every other industrialized country-paying much less for health care while getting the same or better results.

★ 5. Make work pay.
Americans have a right to fair minimum and living wages, to organize and collectively bargain, to enjoy equal opportunity, and to earn equal pay for equal work. Corporate assaults on these rights bring down wages and benefits for all of us. They must be outlawed.

★ 6. Secure social security.
Keep social security sound, and strengthen the retirement, disability, and survivors' protections Americans earn through their hard work. Pay for it by removing the cap on the social security tax, so that upper-income people pay into social security on all they make, just like the rest of us.

★ 7. Return to fairer tax rates.
End, once and for all, the Bush-era tax giveaways for the rich, which the rest of us—or our kids—must pay eventually. Also, we must outlaw corporate tax havens and tax breaks for shipping jobs overseas. Lastly, with millionaires and billionaires taking a growing share of our country's wealth, we should add new tax brackets for those making more than $1 million each year.

★ 8. End the wars and invest at home.
Our troops have done everything that's been asked of them, and it's time to bring them home to good jobs here. We're sending $3 billion each week overseas that we should be investing to rebuild America.

★ 9. Tax Wall Street speculation.
A tiny fee of 1120th of 1 percent on each Wall Street trade would raise tens of billions of dollars annually with little impact on actual investment. This would reduce speculation, "flash trading," and outrageous bankers' bonuses-and we'd have a lot more money to spend on Main Street job creation.

★ 10. Strengthen democracy.
We need clean, fair elections—where no one's right to vote can be taken away, and where money doesn't buy you your own member of Congress. We must ban anonymous political influence, slam shut the lobbyists' revolving door in DC, and publicly finance elections. Immigrants who want to join in our democracy deserve a clear path to citizenship. We must stop giving corporations the rights of people when it comes to our elections. And we must ensure our judiciary's respect for the Constitution. Together, we will reclaim our democracy to get our country back on track.

contract.rebuildthedream.com

Re: Community Lecture

7/19/10 2:31 p.m.
Lecture 9/22/10

Subject: Re: Community Lecture Here they are!

Title: The Absurdity of Capitalism

Description:

As the American and, indeed, the global "free market" capitalist system teeters on the brink of complete collapse and is saved only by the sacrifices of those who least benefit from it; as it drags with it all of society except for the top 10 percent who control 90 percent of all wealth; with American unemployment rates at historic highs, and home foreclosures and generalized bankruptcies proliferating; with American states closing down schools and parks, and shredding our already pitiful "safety net"; with workers worldwide enraged, on the one hand, by their awful treatment under capitalism and, on the other, driven to suicide on the job and as well striking violently for a better deal in nations notorious for harsh repression of such action; as "peak oil" and, indeed, "generalized resource depletion"—ah, yes, all that mineral boodle in Afghanistan!—as all these factors cut the ground out from under the capitalist fantasy of exponential growth in a finite world; and as plans for horrible "resource wars," of "Prequels to Avatar," are being formulated; and, finally, as global climate catastrophe, caused entirely by our irrational economic system and its ruthless exploitation of nature, confronts all who are not willfully blind- with such undeniable challenges and dire consequences confronting us, it is time for us to wake up from the nightmare of capitalist materialism, of gluttonous consumption, of cruel exploitation, and to think forward and work for a social system of democracy and egalitarianism in which the fundamental needs of the immense majority are provided through an economic system devoted, not to private profit, but to human welfare in a way that consciously maintains the ecological basis of our lives.

Gerry Cavanaugh
From Edmond Dantes Vongehr
541-661-5325

Never ever, ever, ever
Sorry, that was then

A few words to ponder as we sail toward the fiscal cliff. Those words would be "That was then, this is now."

Strip away the false piety and legalistic hair splitting offered by republican lawmakers rationalizing their decision to abandon a pledge that they will never ever, ever, ever, vote to raise taxes and that's pretty much what the explanation boils down to.

Rep. Petter Kings says he understood the pledge, propounded by the almighty Grover Norquist and his group Americans for Tax Reform, to obligate him for only one term. Apparently, he thought it had to be renewed, like a driver's license.

Sen. Lindsey Graham says that if Democrats agree to entitlement reform, "I will violate the pledge for the good of the country"—a stirring statement of patriotism and sacrifice that warms your heart like a midnight snack of jalapeño chili fries.

This is not, by the way, a column in defense of the Norquist pledge. The only thing dumber

than his offering such a pledge was scores of politicians sighing it, an opinion that has nothing to do with the wisdom or lack thereof of raising taxes and everything to do with the fact that one ought not, as a matter of simple common sense, make hard, inflexible promises on changeable matters of national import. It is all well and good to stand on whatever one's principles are, but as a politician—a job that, by definition, requires the ability to compromise—you don't needlessly box yourself in. Never say never.

Much less, never ever, ever, ever. So this revolution ___ "he who ___ be ____ ____ ___ __ is nonetheless welcome. It suggests reason seeping like sunlight into places too long cloistered in the damp and dark of ideological rigidity.

But it leaves an observer in the oddly weightless position of applauding weightless position of applauding a thing and being, simultaneously, disgusted by it. Has politics ever seemed more ignoble than in these clumsy, self serving attempts to justify a deviation from orthodoxy? They have to do this, of course, because the truth—"I signed the pledge because I knew it would help me get elected, but with economic ruin looming and Obama re-elected on a promise to raise taxes on the rich and most voters supporting him on that, it's not doing me as much good as it once did"—is unpretty and unflattering.

In this awkward about-face, these lawmakers leave us wondering once again whether the vast majority of them—right and left, red and blue, Republican and Democrat—really believe in anything, beyond being re-elected.

There is a reason congress' approval rating flirted with single digits this year, there is a reason a new Gallup poll finds only 10 percent of Americans ranking congress "high or very high" in honesty and ethics.

Lawyers rank higher. Advertisers rank higher. Even journalists rank higher.

This is the sad pass to which years of congressional grandstanding, fact spinning cookie jar pilfering and assorted harrumphing and pontificating have brought us and while a certain cynicism toward its leading that so many of them are held in plain contempt.

The moral malleability exemplified by the likes of King and Graham will not help. Perhaps we should ask them to sign a new pledge: I will always tell you what I think and what I plan to do in plain English, regardless of whether you like it or it benefits me politically.

But no lawmaker would make that pledge. And who would believe them if they did?

Leonard Pitts Jr., winner of the 2004 Pulitzer Prize for commentary, is a columnist for the Miami Herald.

Your Education Is on This Page

Everything that actually exists in the physical world is a scientific subject. The application of philosophic methods to the real world preceded the scientific method by many centuries, since it was far easier, and required less intelligence, to develop beliefs and opinions than to do the research required in the use of the scientific method.

Science is a method for determining the most probable. This is done by accepting only facts as a criteria of truth.

Philosophy-a combination of beliefs, opinions, prejudice, folklore, traditions, and superstitions, concerning any subject

Fact-a close agreement of a series of careful observations and/or measurements of the same phenomenon able to be repeated

Government-a method of social control

Generally, when one thinks of one's country, and patriotism to it, one thinks of the government-which is only a method. Our country, the USA, is actually some 3.6 million square miles of land area, with all its rivers, soil, forests, mineral resources, along with a few other things, and some 272 million people. When one realizes that, one can't think of patriotism as supporting the waste of natural resources in the production of shoddy goods to increase sales and profits, and one can't have much respect for those who do. One can't support poverty in the midst of plenty, and one can't have much respect for those who do.

Technocracy-the application of the scientific method to the solution of social problems. The scientific method requires careful research from top to bottom of all the physical phenomena concerning whatever subject with which one is concerned. In the case of Technocracy, and the social problems with which our society is faced, we must concern ourselves with humans, the human environment, and the natural laws by which nature requires us to operate. To understand Technocracy is to understand these subjects, at least well enough to understand that, in order to provide solutions for human problems, we must make plans for the future that will conform with nature's requirements. To do otherwise will be a waste of time, at best, and an interference to the continued existence of the human race. For example, we can't continue, forever, increasing the earth's human population with the earth's present natural resources.

Unfortunately, the philosophers and politicians are not prepared, mentally, to understand these problems, or their solutions. They are scientific problems resulting from the enormous scientific progress in recent history in changing the means whereby we live, from an agrarian to a technological operation. And the solutions must be technological operation. And the solutions must be provided by the scientific method.

If one expects to obtain a real education concerning the real physical problems which the human race must face, one can't do better than an in-depth study of Technocracy. A good way to start would be a study of Technocracy's web page-see www.technocracy.org, then contact Technocracy Inc., 2475 Harksell Rd., Ferndale, WA 98248.

—L. W. Nicholson
MAL at Pickens, SC

Money Is a Superstition

Of course, the belief in a monetary, or debt, system is only a superstition. No such thing actually exists in the physical world.

The authors of Technocracy's Study Course Book devoted many pages explaining, in considerable detail, the myth of money.

Beginning on page 121, it explains the concepts of property, trade, value, debt, the flow of money, compound interest, why the purchasing power is not maintained, all these and more, through page 156. That is thirty-five pages, plus another nine pages concerning the operating characteristics of a Price System. A total of fifty-four pages is devoted to explaining a process that is only a myth.

It is obvious that this superstition is the greatest single interference in the progression toward a Technate of North America.

—L. W. Nicholson, MAL

Our Quality of Life Is Being Destroyed

Problems in North America perpetuated by the Price System:

- Overpopulation
- Underemployment increasing as technology expands
- Food banks on the increase
- Violence ever with us
- Robberies ever with us and ongoing
- Drugs out of control
- Forest disappearing much too rapidly
- Rivers and streams polluted, hazardous specially to fish
- Mining extraction-toxic waste problem
- Shortage of money for schooling
- Ever-increasing spread between rich and poor
- Health services in trouble
- Much of our infrastructure in trouble
- Severe automobile congestion
- Public transit sadly lacking
- University fees extremely high
- Many fish strains gone forever
- Energy-saving passenger trains losing out
- Politicians out of date in our modern high-tech age
- Employment insurance a real problem
- Tourism far overdone, causing extreme congestion and major pollution

— Seldom in our early days did we lock our doors; now we bolt them and many have expensive security systems
— Vast number of clam and oyster beds polluted Crab fishing areas diminished
— River foreshores extensively gone to industry, destroying access and natural flow
— Our planet's species are disappearing rapidly
— A number of ski hills damaging the environment
— Junk mail keeps piling up at our doors
— Many streets now unsafe to walk
— Much of our agricultural land lost to wrong enterprises, leading to a shortage of acreage
— Our Canadian Broadcasting (CBC) programs diminishing-cash strapped
— Our general police forces short of finances
— Jet planes with their fifty tons of fuel (extravagance) polluting our delicate planet
— Prostitution and pimping employing children-sad
— Schoolchildren now escorted to school, unsafe otherwise
— Third-world immigration adding to our diseases
— Roads and bridges wearing out fast now with added population
— Petty crime up-purse snatching in vogue
— Interest rates erratic
— Crank telephone calls

And so on with our archaic economy. Technocracy's economic program is a blueprint for conservation in sync with our high-tech era. Our current system, namely, a Price System, has caused very serious trouble in nearly every aspect. The scientific society Technocracy proposes will save us and planet earth for two to three thousand years.

Ralph Lundahl
Technocracy member at our British Columbia section, Aldergrove

It is the part of a good shepherd to
shear his flock, not to skin it.

2/10/98

Dear Mosie:

Thanks for your items on the money problems of the world. To my way of thinking, basically money (dollars, marks, yen, pesos, or whatever) are supposed to be a means of fair exchange for goods or services whether domestic or foreign.

One of the problems, probably the main problem, is that money does not have an intrinsic value. Until a different method is used to establish a countrywide true value for goods and services that does not fluctuate and not subject to manipulations of any kind, there will never be a solution to the greed factors inherent in the means of exchange. As long as it is based on what the technologists call our price system, based on no fixed or static value and subject to too many variables, none the least of which is the immoral fact that money and the holders thereof can influence the very lives of the whole nation or other nations. This applies whether the transaction is between individuals, companies, or international.

If only people would study the many facts as researched by the scientists, economists and engineers of Technocracy Inc. for twelve years during the 1920s and early '30s, twelve years of intensive scientific conclusions based on facts, not fiction, that would solve and will solve most all if not all of our present social problems through education and knowledge of ways to overhaul our system to produce so much goods and services, that every person on our North American continent would have the means to have the equivalent, at their annual disposal, of what $80,000.00 of today's money value (2/10/98) would represent. These figures are facts, not dreams. In my lifetime I have known quite a few very wealthy millionaires and the amazing thing about them personally, was that they were all quite frugal in their personal habits as to their dietary, food, clothing, recreation, etc. You can only eat so much per day, wear so many clothes, do so many things etc. These people being of normal or higher intelligence, given a choice, could trade their present worries and concerns, fears, anxieties, and all the negatives of life, for a world of security, both personal, financial, etc. and that of their families and heirs to follow for generations to come only need open their minds and hearts and be willing to study the answers formulated by Technocracy, Inc. over the past seventy years. And when enough people become aware of the way things are now and why the present political and economic system that is controlled and driven by money has caused most if not all the ills of our society. Dear Moser: I am enclosing a copy of "The Energy Certificate" that tells how the money problem could be solved.

Also a copy of "History and Purpose of Technocracy." And if this stirs any interest in that beautiful mind of yours, I have many more publications that will answer any questions or doubts you might have regarding the changes necessary in our society.

Your Gramps: in the search for truth.
Love,
E. D. V.

CHQ, Technocracy Inc.
Ferndale, Washington
February 4, 2004

Well, it has been a strange year on this part of the globe. The actions of our political and business leadership have been rather frantic in trying to maintain the illusion of a stable economic and social scene. In part because of the election coming next year, and in part because they must convince people that losing their jobs is necessary, that they must sacrifice a bit as the global economic model takes hold. Oh, about actually moving the factories abroad thus losing not only jobs, but any chance of finding another? Retraining is the key. You bet.

Whole towns are being shuttered closed. We see this as almost a weekly event in the news. Men and women dropping off the unemployment lines as their benefits expire. This does make the statistical job market look good though. We see George W. Bush strutting around—so proud because his tax cuts are working!

We could go on for pages about the political and business abuses and excuses. Wall Street. Some states in the US going broke. And then there is the Bush proposal to give some kind of reprieve to all the illegal immigrants in the US. Trouble is, after six years they have to leave, to be replaced by other illegal workers who may settle for even lower wages. As we know, in a technocracy this would not happen. The area we call Mexico would benefit as part of the continental operations. I would venture a guess that most of the people immigrating would prefer to live in their home area and only move on to try and better their plight. The political leadership in Mexico seeks no change of policy that would help the common citizen. Of course the overriding problem here, and affecting the entire world, is overpopulation. Not enough can be said to emphasize this. Nothing will be done about the population problem until a technocracy is installed because the Price System requires an expanding population base to survive.

Maybe some of the same things are happening in Canada. We do watch the TV news from there, but if it anything like the media in the US, we are lucky to get even some correct information. And so it goes. But all this is really just Price System machinations. To some degree, it is just history repeating itself. How many wars have been started to give the economy a boost and grab or steal resources? We can waste a lot of mental effort getting all worked up about all of this, and that just takes us away from our most important job of being members of Technocracy.

We have a suggestion for those who have the time and inclination. Become regional CHQs. Take on projects that mean something. For instance, get a list of the school districts in your area and send some info to the social studies or a related department. Put your name and address as a return contact. Filter out the responses, if any. Talk to them. Let them know of our website. If they are serious, they will contact us through the Web's e-mail system, telephone (we now have a toll-free number: 1-800-797-2711) or by old-fashioned mail. Use your imagination and find people. We have shelves loaded with briefs and article reprints that we will send you gratis. We will get one more shot at the goal for which this organization was established and we should do all we can.

A bright spot: Ron Miller, our authorized speaker from Portland, and an associate of Technocracy, Mark Ciotola, lecturer from the San Francisco State University, will be attending two (so far) economic conferences this year: one in Salt Lake City in April, the other in Denver during the month of September. They intend to hit hard at the impossibility of the Price System's demand for continual expansion. They will state as clearly as possible that there is no other alternative but what the gifted men and women of the Technical Alliance concluded from their scientific research: that if we have any hope of a future worth living, we must adopt Technocracy's design of scientific functional governance.

There is also another bright spot in visually helping people get into and around the wealth information Technocracy has available and that can be accessed with their fingertips on a keyboard. Bill Des Jardines in Edmonton, Alberta, has established an exciting website for Technocracy. It can be found at www.Technocracy.ca. Take a look and be sure to let your contacts know of the site.

And speaking of Edmonton, we have a very active group in that area headed by Walt Fryers, an organizer. Walt also contributes articles for the *North American Technocrat*. Ross Deacon, a member of the group, calls CHQ several times throughout the year and offers suggestions and lets us know what is going on there in Edmonton.

Ron Miller's group in Portland is welcoming new members and the section in San Francisco is another area that is doing its best to keep current. They have encouraged Mark Ciotola with his lecturing of

Technocracy's information about thermodynamics and the three curve chart. We also have to give a note of appreciation to Caryl and Richard Burnett snuggled away out there in Arkansas. They track down so many good sources for material in the magazine that my mail system gets overloaded. We can speak of these things because we receive feedback from members who are contributing. So please feel free to do the same for any of your individual programs that might otherwise go unrecognized.

In an attempt to garner more interest in Technocracy, there will be a series of ads placed in strategic newspapers and magazines. This is extremely expensive. We do have some funds set aside for this project, but the rates we have to pay for even a simple ad will make the money disappear very quickly. At the very least, donations of any amounts will be greatly appreciated and put to good use.

We have been at the job of updating our "Energy Certificate" booklet for some time. It is now complete and a copy is included with this letter. You will notice that the title has been changed to the "Energy Distribution Card." It was felt that it reflected a more accurate description than "Certificate" or "Debit" card. We would have had a much more difficult time if not for Fem McFarlane's and John Darvill's initiating the upgrading procedure.

CHQ also would have a much more difficult time if not for the helpful visits of both Fem and Ralph Raab. Fem is from Michigan and Ralph is from Ontario. The one person who is the glue that holds everything together, Grace Sheldon, along with the staffing duties of Paul Cordsmeyer, makes it possible for us to continue to operate from CHQ. Amy Wright does a most valuable job in helping with office work for the *North American Technocrat* magazine.

We also must give a large salute to the very fine members across the border who come every quarter and help assemble and mail out our magazine. They now have the added indignity of dealing with the surly border guards.

In closing, maybe we should discuss the one thought that we as members must have in common. That thought is "Even if we are successful in bringing to the attention of the public, the need for functional governance, will our environment and social installations be so damaged that nothing will help?" It could tum out that way, we just do not know for sure. The fact that we do not know is reason enough to keep slugging it out. The question we should be asking is "What else can we do with our lives?" We know too much—we have been witness to the gradual and now accelerating harm to our planet, and we know that any other concept or organizational effort to change all this is an effort in futility. We may not make it, but we have to go down trying. We owe it to ourselves and to all the other great people who came before us in this organization we call Technocracy.

We at CHQ bid you all a very healthy and eventful New Year.

—George Wright

Gloom and Despair among Advocates of the Poor

By David Firestone
IN NEW YORK Poverty-Welfare
NY Times, Sept. 21, 1995

T he morning after the Senate voted to end the country's 60-year-old guarantee of relief for poor families, a group of people who have devoted their careers to those families gathered in a tired public-housing assembly room in Manhattan yesterday for one of the gloomiest meetings any of them could remember.

The directors of the city's 37 settlement houses, which provide charitable services to more than half a million low-income people every year, were stunned by the Senate's action, and particularly by the strong bipartisan support behind it. There were calls for prayer at their monthly meeting, and there were fears of riots voiced.

Like dozens of others in New York who spend every working day among the nation's largest welfare population, several said they were gripped by a sense of despair that the social contract had finally crumpled-along with a national sense of hope and compassion that once lent honor to their profession.

"I'm 63 years old, and I've worked here since 1957, and I don't remember a moment that's been worse," said Eugene Sklar, executive director of the Union Settlement, a charitable institution in East

Harlem founded 100 years ago. "Even during the Great Depression, there was a sense that people cared enough to tum it around. But now, the prevailing public attitude views those at the lowest rungs of society as responsible for the country's problems. It's madness."

"I don't remember a moment that's been worse," said a Settlement House director.

There has been a hazy sense of foreboding among poor people and their advocates since the Republican Party gained control of Congress last November. For many, though, the vote in the Senate on Tuesday was the first staggering blow, the most serious indicator of how lives and hopes will now begin to change as welfare benefits are reduced and strict limits to public assistance are imposed.

There were widespread predictions of an increase in homelessness and crime, along with warnings that more children would go hungry with a cut in food stamp benefits. Liz Krueger, associate director of the Community Food Resource Center in Manhattan, said the broad new discretion given the states under the welfare bill would induce the states to compete to offer the lowest welfare benefits. Especially in combination with the profound changes in social services already under way at the city and state levels, the welfare vote seemed to many social workers a shudder in the progress of time.

"We're going back to the poorhouse mentality, to before the new deal," said Daniel Kronenfeld, who runs the 102-year-old Henry Street Settlement on the Lower East Side. "We've all seen hard times before. But what's frightening about this is that it's so broad, on so many levels of government. The entire country seems to think that everything we've tried has failed."

The Senate welfare bill, which appears to have the tentative backing of President Clinton, would put a five-year time-limit on welfare benefits, and would require that half of all recipients be working by the year 2000. Most dramatically, it would end the Federal guarantee of assistance to families that meet eligibility requirements, and instead substitute lump-sum payments to states for distribution.

A similar work requirement began earlier this year for thousands of public assistance recipients without children in New York City, along with stringent new eligibility requirements that the city says will remove 100,000 people from the welfare rolls by year's end.

Though Mayor Rudolph W. Giuliani has been critical of the tougher welfare bill passed by the House because it would cut off aid to mothers who have more children while on welfare, he praised the approach of the Senate bill yesterday.

"Generally, I favor the Senate approach to the way in which welfare reform should be done, and that is similar to what we're doing in practicality here in New York City," he said at a news conference. "You put the emphasis on work, workfare, getting people back to work and into work situations realistically as fast as you can."

But in New York, most people in the workfare program are cleaning litter from parks and performing other routine tasks, and Ms. Krueger said they are not learning the kinds of job skills that could prepare them for full-time employment.

Though the approach has now been endorsed by the President and the vast majority of the Democrats in the Senate, she said it would not solve the problem that politicians trying to change the welfare program are trying to fix.

"Workfare is the opposite of work," she said. "It makes people work for less than the minimum wage, with no benefits or opportunity for advancement, and it lowers the wages of the employed. They continue to fixate on the question of why poor people won't go to work, when the real question is, why aren't there jobs for poor people?"

That sentiment was echoed yesterday by several welfare recipients interviewed outside a city welfare office at 14th Street and Fifth Avenue. Any change in the welfare program that might help them get meaningful jobs would be welcomed, they said, but they remained skeptical about that being the real intent.

Calls for prayer and fears of riots are among the reactions to welfare legislation.

"I can live with the time period, if something beneficial is down the road," said Jeffrey Bullard, 37, a Staten Island resident. "But if you look for the cup of gold at the end of the rainbow, it probably won't be there."

Verlondia Gardner, a 32-year-old mother of four who lives in a Lower East Side housing project and has been on welfare for 10 years, said the only welfare reform she wanted was a job.

"If they are going to help you benefit yourself so you can get off, that will be good," she said. "I want to get me more work, a job, something so I can get off. I would really like to."

Nancy Wackstein, executive director of the Lenox Hill Neighborhood House on the Upper East Side, said many advocates agreed that there were flaws and over-regulation in the current welfare system. But the changes now being proposed, she said, would cause far more problems than they fixed. In particular, she said, moving control of welfare toward the states is a step backward.

"Before the Federal Government got involved, the states never assumed enough responsibility for these issues," she said. "If everything were left to the states, there would be no civil rights, no environmental protection. Some things have to be left to the Federal Government."

New York State faces a particular problem in the debate over Medicaid and welfare because its programs are among the biggest and most generous, and the state has a long tradition of doing more for poor people.

New York City, in particular, has high concentrations of poor people, greater numbers of people with expensive diseases like AIDS and tuberculosis and a high cost of living.

In Albany, however, officials in the Pataki Administration said they had settled on no firm plans on how they would absorb the cuts proposed in the House or Senate bills. Whichever welfare bill is passed, they said, could ultimately speed up their own efforts to cut each program, efforts that the Assembly Democrats watered down considerably in the state budget fight earlier this year.

The proposals originally made by Gov. George E. Pataki included time limits as short as 60 days for people receiving Home

Relief—the program primarily for able-bodied adults without children—and reduced welfare grants for women with children.

The state is also considered likely to follow the city's lead and expand its workfare programs and its eligibility reviews.

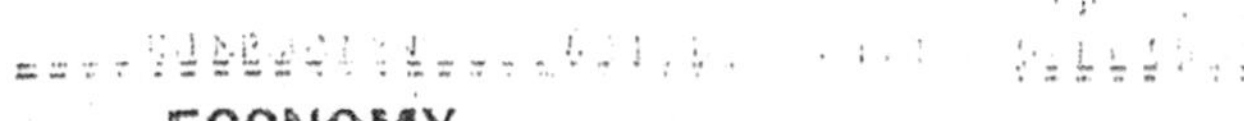

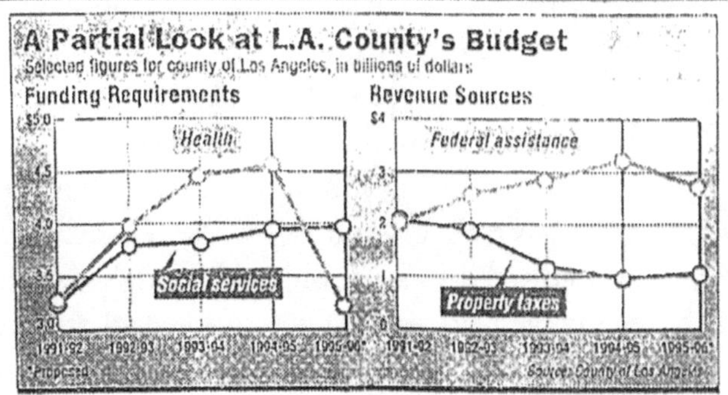

Los Angeles County to Begin Downsizing By Issuing 5,200 Layoffs, Demotions

By Frederick Rose
Staff Reporter of the Wall Street Journal

L O ANGELES—About 5,200 layoffs and demotions will be issued to Los Angeles health-care workers today in what analysts say is the first of many moves that will downsize government in the nation's most populous county.

The reductions are needed to close a revenue decline of over $1 billion and will be accompanied by the Oct. 1 closing of dozens of clinics and other services counted on by the county's 2.6 million residents who are without health insurance and 1.8 million Medicaid patients.

Los Angeles County is a patchwork of some 80 cities, the largest of which is the city of Los Angeles, with a population of more than three million people. The county has a total population of more than 9.4 million people. Its budget is by far the nation's largest at the county level.

Shaken by earthquake, riot, fire and its deepest economic downturn since the Great Depression, Los Angeles County's finances have weakened year by year, analysts say. In a region where climbing real-estate values were once a tradition, the county assessor recently reported a $10.2 billion plunge, to $487 billion, in the county's total assessed value. It was the first such drop in 22 years.

Los Angeles County's newly emerging fiscal difficulties—unlike those of neighboring Orange County, whose December filing for bankruptcy was sparked by $1.7 billion in high-risk investment losses—is the result of fundamental economic and structural problems, analysts say. And, unlike Orange County, which has resisted giant service cutbacks, Los Angeles County is bracing for sharp reductions.

Even so, the fiscal fate of these neighboring counties may be closely tied by last-minute political maneuvering in the California legislature, where Los Angeles area representatives have fought to ally a $50 million transfer of transportation funds to approval of a similar but far bigger and more complicated package for Orange County. Despite the turmoil, political insiders expect the Orange County package to be approved.

Today's cuts in Los Angeles are but the first. In addition to health-care layoffs, the county yesterday said it expects to terminate or demote more than 800 probation officers.

Thousands more layoffs among the county health department's 27,000 employees may follow if last-ditch efforts fail to raise hundreds of millions of state and federal dollars. A county spokeswoman yesterday described those efforts as "looking very gloomy."

Los Angeles administrators and outsiders are openly concerned about effects ranging from increased risks of epidemics to violent protests among the city's poor. "The drastic curtailments," in health services needed to narrow some $655 million of the county's overall shortfall" will have devastating consequences on all residents of Los Angeles County," concluded the task force that recommended them.

"We're talking about literally turning people away from health care by the thousands," said Raphael Sonenshein, a political scientist and visiting scholar at the University of Southern California. "I don't think anyone is prepared for this."

The task force estimated that clinic closures will cut off about 1.9 million patient visits or a little more than half of this past year's total visits. Health department officials said that adjustments made since those estimates will cut the number of visits further.

County officials are negotiating with private providers about joint projects intended to cover some county needs. However, the details and extent of those arrangements aren't yet known. The county's newly named "health czar," Burt Margolin, said a first contract is expected next week. As for the hospitals, "what we are facing here is not a restructuring but a sudden-death closure syndrome," Mr. Margolin said.

Los Angeles County's problems are the result of rising costs of welfare and health care for an expanding, poor population, as well as sharply curtailed state transfers to the county budget, analysts said. And, like much else in California's arcane fiscal structure, the problems derive from 1977's tax-slashing Proposition 13.

Starting in the fiscal year ended June 30, 1993, the state shifted more than $1 billion of property tax receipts from the county to schools and community college systems within it. The state, in turn, shifted some sales taxation power to the county. But those receipts were far smaller. In a county budget which peaked at $11.91 billion in the June 30, 1995, fiscal year just ended, these cuts were a blow. "The economy itself was causing enough problems, but then the state imposed an even bigger one," noted Kenneth Kurtz, a vice president at Moody's Investors Service.

The county, however, covered these shortages with a variety of one-time adjustments, accounting shifts, asset sales, and federal funds. With the latest budget, however, these arrangements came to an end. "They've run out of one-time items," said Mr. Kurtz.

Fascism Growing in North America

Most of us are concerned about the increase in hate, violence, the growth of the religious right, the wide popularity of right-wing broadcasters, the spread of the militia movements. Usual prescription: crackdown. More police, more jails, stiffer criminal sentences.

But these are the symptoms. Outgrowths of the basic problem middle-class malaise. Most North Americans are in the middle class, neither super-rich nor desperately poor.

Let's recognize the reasons for middle-class concerns. And let's recognize that unless those concerns are properly addressed, we could be heading into fascism!

First, let's compare what's been happening in the US during the past decade, with what happened in Europe some decades earlier. Understand cause and effect. Note the similarities. Only then will we know what to do about what's happening in our society. And recognize the imminent danger to our democracy.

How Fascism Began

Before WWI, several right-wing French writers, notably Georges Sorel and Charles Maurras, and the Italian Gabriele D'Annunzio, extolled the superiority of big business. They called for a strong capitalist state under big business management. Then all would be well.

But their ideas got little support from politicians until economic and social malaise set in among the middle class. First, it happened in Italy. An Italian Marxist, editor of a socialist newspaper (*Avanti*) named Benito Mussolini, was intrigued by D'Annunzio's confidence in big business to set everything right. Mussolini quickly switched from far left to far right.

Switching from one extreme to the other is not uncommon. Our Ronald Reagan used to be a leftist liberal Democrat, supported Helen Gahagan Douglas in California (Nixon called her a Red) and in the 1948 presidential campaign, he was to the left of Harry Truman. He thought Truman wasn't liberal enough and backed Truman's challenger, leftist Henry Wallace, for the Democratic nomination. Then one day he switched, moved from left to right. We know the rest of the story.

But back to Mussolini. His idols were D'Annunzio, Sorel, and the German philosopher Nietzsche, who glorified "action" and "vitality." In 1919, Mussolini invented the term fascism. Inspired by the ancient Roman power symbol, the fasces—a bundle of sticks tied to an ax—to show "unity" and the power of the state to punish dissenters.

Fascism in Italy

After WWI, postwar depression was particularly hard on the middle class. Joblessness, insecurity, shattered dreams. Workers went on strike in the cities, peasants on the farms. Mussolini, the new fascist leader, called on big business to finance a crackdown. Agricultural landowners, the Roman Catholic Church and the army, gave strong support-in the name of "fighting the red wave." They argued that those horrible red leftists were responsible for the strikes.

Like Hitler who came later in Germany, Mussolini was a charismatic orator, a powerful demagogue. His backers, big business—urban and rural—along with the church and the army, staged a coup, making him dictator of Italy. (Note the similarity with traditional oligarchic triumvirates in Latin America, landowners, church, and military, supported by the politicians. They put the politicians into power and the politicians kept them in power.) That's the way it was in Italy under Mussolini.

He promptly announced: all strikes strictly forbidden, all labor unions abolished, all political opposition silenced. Called himself Il Duce, the Leader (Hitler later emulated and called himself Der Fuhrer).

Understand the technique: repress the poor, enrich the rich, fascinate the middle class. With oratory, theatrics, "law and order," and simplistic promises. The trains ran on time.

The Great Depression

Came the Great Depression of the late 1920s and early '30s. Il Duce had no program for solving social and economic problems, except to give free rein to big business. Then wealth would "trickle down." And he preached the need for "family values," "discipline," and "faith."

As a result, Italian workers lost their jobs, lost their eight-hour workday, and in addition, Mussolini cut their wages. Real wages in Italy went down by half. By 1930, they were the lowest in all of Western Europe. On instructions from farm owners, he forbade migration to the cities. That forced farmhands to stay on the farm, while their purchasing power declined by as much as 70 percent. Result: Happy farm owners—they could keep wages low. Their employees were forbidden to complain, forbidden to leave. Slave labor.

Child labor laws were abolished, so little children could be forced to work, social services cut ("balance the budget!"). Peasants were sharecroppers; the rich owned the farms. Mussolini, of course, did nothing to break up the latifondi—their big estates. (Just fifteen rich families owned over a million acres of the best land in Italy.) Health care declined. Infant mortality was over twice as high as in Scandinavia.

In a word, Mussolini's formula for dealing with the Great Depression was to enrich the wealthy, enslave the poor, and encourage everybody to increase the birth rate. More personnel for labor and military service. That demonstrated "vitality," he said.

Finally, to get people's minds off their woes, he began conquest of foreign lands. Moved into Libya and into Ethiopia. Fanned patriotism, with cries for Nice, Corsica, Djibouti! Hitler copied that too, crying, "Wie lange ohne Kolonien?" (How long without colonies?)

Antifeminism

Intriguing, how today's antifeminism of our religious right echoes Mussolini. With his emphasis on "family values," he argued that it was the duty of women to stay home and bear as many children as possible. (Again—Hitler adopted that very same program in Germany.)

In 1940, Mussolini staged a parade in Rome of 180 married couples who'd produced 1,440 children, eight per couple. He gave all the mothers gold medals for "service to the nation."

Women were excluded from white-collar jobs, denied formal education, so they could stay home and have more babies. Birth control, of course, was strictly banned. Anyone offering birth control information was tossed into the clink, immediately.

One of Il Duce's top fascist propagandists, Ferdinando Loffredo, wrote, "Women must return under the subjection of man—father or husband—and must recognize therefore her own spiritual, cultural, and economic inferiority." Mussolini fervently agreed.

Fascists, not only in Germany but in France, echoed the Italian theme. They began identifying demands for sexual equality as a "Marxist class struggle." French novelist Pierre Drieu La Rochelle called feminism "a pernicious doctrine" because women did not have the spiritual qualities of men and dragged men down to decadence.

How It Worked

Mussolini's dictatorship caused a big decline in the nutrition of the poorer people, forced more of their young children out of school and into the workforce, relegated women to the bedroom, and extolled the military. War was "virtuous." "Nothing has ever been won in history without bloodshed!" And he promoted the slogan "Believe! Obey! Fight!"

The Italian male was to be tough, not "soft" and "humanitarian." Gays were ridiculed as "decadent," and individualism must be replaced by nationalism. Social services cut to the bone.

As for religion, Mussolini signed Lateran Accords with the Vatican, establishing Roman Catholicism as the only state religion.

Consumers, small business, were neglected, while big business formed cartels and monopolized the economy.

That's how fascism began, in Italy. Sound familiar?

April 29, 2005, Trendevents

Welcome, all, to the new Trendevents! We received a wonderfully informative letter from ex-member Clyde Wilson. Thank you Clyde for sending such a fine assortment of very useful and interesting articles! Have you considered becoming an active member again? Our newsletter and the *North American Technocrat* magazine could use input from all willing to participant in this endeavor. Many thanks to members Richard and Caryl Burnett for the many useful email articles they provide on a regular daily basis.

Mr. Wilson participated as valuable member of Section 2, for forty-five years in Los Angeles. He named the original monthly research bulletin Trendevents. Several members including Clyde, at Section 2, wrote for the Trendevents, including Wilton Ivie and Howard Scott from CHQ in Rushland, Pa. Jessie Barns did the typing, and members of Section 2 ran it off on the mimeograph and all pitched in the mailing. A Big Technocracy Salute to all members, living and passed, who over the past seventy-plus years, have given countless hours of their time and money to keep our organization functioning into the twenty-first century. Paul C.

The Basics of Technocracy

Technocrat L. W. Nicholson: Some things change very slowly, in fact at speeds, which seen to be the next thing to zero. The motions of the Earth's crust, plate tectonics, for example. The laws of thermo-dynamics and gravitation may be expected to be the same in the next century, as well as the last. Energy flows from the sun, some finds the earth in its path, and part of that is absorbed by the earth. It is the difference between this and the amount which is reflected back into space that provides the energy to grow all the earth's plants and animals, the cause of the winds and the rains which fall, as well as most of the other earth processes to occur. It is these processes and their dependability that keeps the earth from being in a state of chaos.

A comparison of scientific laws vs. manmade laws and regulations science is a study of these processes, and what makes science more accurate than other manmade methods is the determination to allow only that which can be verified to be considered a fact.

Social Conditions Effected By Technocrat Ron Miller: A Price System must have continuous expansion. This means that every enterprise, no matter what it does, must increase its profits continually. At the moment, our entire society is geared up to sell everything to everyone. Shopping has become a major avocation. What would our society look like if there were no longer any reason to advertise goods just to add more to the bottom line? What would happen if people were instead to become really aware of what high rates of consumption of natural resources is doing to their world?

Science Is Concerned with Proven Facts

With no price system, things suddenly become much simpler. All you have to do then is keep all the technology running that keeps us all alive. Something like 95 percent of all laws becomes pointless and therefore non-operative. What is really necessary is to distribute the goods that people want. The people who would do this are doing it now. The only real difference is that most of the people in the front office would no longer be needed. Selection to fill vacant positions would, mostly, be made from within. Those in the positions that report to the vacant position would select from among their group several people that they felt were qualified to hold that position and those to whom the vacant position reports would pick the best of those selected (from their point of view). If, after a time, it appears that the person selected is not working out as planned, another could be selected.

People have accused Technocracy of being undemocratic because of this process. My favorite example is that when an airliner is about to take off, what would one think if the passengers were required to elect the pilot from among their group? Personally I don't care who the pilot is so long as he has been tested and proven qualified. One thing that I have become a great fan of, is the environmental impact statement. Every possible effect of a project is examined at length with the views of all carefully considered and weighed.

On What Planet Do Bush and Co. Live? Seattle Post-Intelligencer
04/26/05
Paul Krugman

According to John Snow, the Treasury secretary, the global economy is in a "sweet spot." Conservative pundits close to the administration talk, without irony, about a "Bush boom." Yet two-thirds of Americans polled by Gallup say that the economy is "only fair" or "poor." And only 33 percent of those polled believe the economy is improving, while 59 percent think it's getting worse.

Is the administration's obliviousness to the public's economic anxiety just partisanship? I don't think so: President Bush and other Republican leaders honestly think that we're living in the best of times. After all, everyone they talk to these days says so . . . What's going on? Actually, it's quite simple: Bush and his party talk only to their base-corporate interests and the religious right-and are oblivious to everyone else's concerns.

The administration's upbeat view of the economy is a case in point. Corporate interests are doing very well. As a recent report from the Center on Budget and Policy Priorities points out, over the past three years profits grew at an average rate 14.5 percent after inflation, the fastest growth since World War II.

The story is very different for the great majority of Americans, who live off their wages, not dividends or capital gains, and aren't doing well at all. Over the past three years, wage and salary income grew less than in any other postwar recovery-less than a tenth as fast as profits. But wage-earning Americans aren't part of the base . . .

According to CBS, only 25 percent of the public have confidence in Bush's ability to make the right decisions about Social Security; 70 percent are "uneasy." The point is that people sense, correctly, that Bush doesn't understand their concerns. He was sold on privatization by people who have made their careers in the self-referential, corporate-sponsored world of conservative think tanks. And he himself has no personal experience with the risks that working family's face. He's probably never imagined what it would be like to be destitute in his old age, with no guaranteed income . . .

It all makes you wonder how these people ever ended up running the country in the first place. But remember that in 2000, Bush pretended to be a moderate, and that in the next two elections he used the Iraq war as a wedge to divide and perplex the Democrats . . .

Democracy Corps, the Democratic pollsters, say that there is a crisis of confidence in the Republican direction for the country. As they're careful to point out, this won't necessarily translate into a surge of support for Democrats.

But Americans . . . are worried about a weak job market, soaring health care costs, rising oil prices and a war that seems to have no end. And they're starting to notice that nobody in power is even trying to deal with these problems, because the people in charge are too busy catering to a base that has other priorities.

Reality Can't be Altered or Ignored Atlanta Journal Constitution
04/22/05
By Jay Bookman

If you can't change reality, change the perception of reality. Global Terrorism, the annual report that since 1985 has compiled how many major terror incidents occur each year. As you may recall, that report gained a certain notoriety during last year's presidential campaign, after the State Department announced that the number of terrorist attacks declined in 2003. Bush administration officials quickly cited the finding as vindication for their anti-terror policies, until it was discovered that the report had somehow left out hundreds of terror attacks. In reality, the number of attacks had increased in 2003, not declined.

Given that embarrassment-and the fact that the report for 2004 would reportedly have shown another increase-the report was made to vanish. That fits a pattern. When the number of mass layoffs announced around the country began to be a political problem, the Bush Labor Department simply stopped collecting that data.

When governors complained about inadequate funding, citing a document called "Budget Information for States," the White House stopped publishing that document, too. Spokesman Trent Duffy said at the time that the change was necessary to reduce the cost of "paper and producing another volume."

These days, more than two years into the Iraq war, the Bush administration still refuses to include the mounting costs of the war in its official budget, insisting that it be treated as an emergency expenditure. That way, the cost of the war isn't included in the official estimate of the federal budget deficit.

That particular game has become so obvious-and so embarrassing, even to some Republicans-that the US Senate voted 61-31 this week to urge the Bush administration to be more forthright in its budget. But that won't happen.

You see, it's hard to reduce our huge budget deficit. You'd have to raise taxes and cut spending. It's a lot easier to just change the perception. Likewise, it's a lot easier to eliminate a report on terrorism than to eliminate terrorism.

The problem, of course, is that perception is not reality. Reality exists independent of whatever perception we care to create about it. If the money spent in Iraq isn't reflected in the official deficit figures, does that somehow make our budget reality any better?

If there are no pictures of dead American soldiers being returned to this country for burial, did they not really die?

If the White House promises Congress that a new Medicare drug benefit will cost no more than $400 billion-and threatens to fire government analysts if they tell the truth, that the real cost will be closer to $530 billion-does that mean taxpayers won't have to pay the bill of $720 billion, which is the latest reality-based estimate?

If study after study proves that abstinence-only education doesn't work and may actually backfire, can we pretend away the increased number of pregnancies, abortions, and cases of HIV likely to result?

Every administration tries to manipulate public perception, but this is something different. In many cases, this administration actually believes in the false reality it tries so hard to create. It weaves an illusion around itself of how the world really works, then makes policy based on that illusion.

In time, that must inevitably lead to big trouble. It already has in Iraq-you know, that country that was filled with weapons of mass destruction, ready to greet us with open arms, able to finance its own reconstruction?-and it will do so again.

It is impossible for anyone, either as individuals or as nations, to have a complete and accurate grasp on reality. The best we can ever do is guess and be willing to adjust our concept of reality based on new information. But to the Bush administration, those adjustments to reality are signs of weakness. Its working principle is that if reality doesn't conform to ideology, it is reality that must be altered, because the ideology is fixed and not to be questioned. In the short term, that can pay political benefits. But in the long run, you pay a serious price if you let your perception of reality diverge too far from reality itself.

A weeklong series on Boston's NPR station, WBUR, titled "Addicted to Oil." This report was posted on the Energy Resources List by Dick Lawrence.

NY Times' Thomas Friedman's new book, The World Is Flat. The title refers to the enormous leveling of the playing field brought about by globalization and high-bandwidth telecom capabilities that enable just about any high-tech and white-collar job to be done from anywhere, to the benefit of lower-cost labor centers like Bangalore.

Mr. Jay Franklin and many others protest that Technocracy means the surrender of personal liberty. What liberty has the average man left to surrender? Last year, the government took one-fourth of every citizen's money. This year's income tax promises to take the skin off any prosperity anybody may have chanced upon.

Even religious freedom is still largely restricted to certain powerful sects. Everywhere we turn, today, we find our liberty surrendered.

If Technocracy could even approximate its vision of $20,000 a year for eight hours' work a week, it would be offering 79 percent liberty in place of the present 10 percent, or less. Twenty thousand a year would be liberty almost unallowed.

Mr. Franklin speaks of "tyranny" of the group of scientists who would gain "absolute power of life and death over this nation." But, in the first place, the scientists would be busy improving the knowledge, the power, the health, and the happiness of mankind. The governors elected, responsible, accountable, impeachable, and surely no more capable of tyranny than the political bosses who have made our judiciary, our public finances, our politics the ghastly mockeries they are, today.

While it is certain that government would be altered almost beyond recognition in the process of adoption of Technocracy, let nobody pretend that this would be any greater, or more radical a revolution, than a dozen that have already taken place in this nation of ours.

The idea of equality of income seems insane to many. Yet our idea of taxing the rich heavily and the poor not at all, and the increasing severity of inheritance taxes, and the like, tend to bring the two classes closer. Today, the poor, the common people, have all the power in their hands and can vote anything they will. And they are most ominously interested in Technocracy. They have listened for three years to the tragic-comic statements of the great financial geniuses. They have heard "just around the corner" turned into a pitiful bit of old slang.

Among the loudest ridiculers of Technocracy is one who calls it "Utopian nonsense." He is one of those who make a business of telling just what is going to happen; when it does not happen he goes blandly on, telling just what is going to happen next. A year ago, I heard him guarantee, oracularly, that prosperity would be here in six months.

A Technocratic suggestion for money is a receipt to the citizen for services rendered, instead of a claim against the state. Technocratic money would be a debt paid, a balance in the bank, instead of a mortgage on the government. It might not work. Nothing ever works as planned. But it would be a funny kind of money, indeed, if it could work less satisfactorily than our present system.

This country owes itself over 200 billion dollars. The so-called civilized world owes itself 400 billion-far more than it is worth. It is bankrupt, busted. Fortunately, we can have "prosperity" by hysteria as well as panic by it. Let us hope we may soon have another boom, but how long will it be before it also goes "boom"?

People who have once been rich and hope to be, again, look with horror or derision on the Technocratic notion of equality of income. Now, I cannot imagine equality of character. But I am nevertheless utterly convinced that equality of opportunity and equality in freedom of thought, speech, votes are truly inborn and inalienable.

And I can now believe that, in a human sense, approximate economic equality is not only infinitely desirable but also practical and possible. This does not mean equality of power, influence, prestige, or glory. There must always be reward for ambition and toil and skill.

But what sort of man can he be who could really want to maintain the present system of a few having all the luxury and the vast majority the drudgery, a few the cream, the rest only skim milk? I am as far as possible from being an anarchist, or a communist, or a socialist. But it warms my heart, as no other dream has ever done, to imagine everybody having the dread of poverty removed, the hideous torments of anxiety gone, and the gates of leisure and a little luxury opened.

Mr. Franklin asks about international relations, in case we were Technocrats in a non-Technocratic world. This is a problem to be met, but it is futile to demand, today, a guaranteed foolproof, hole proof solution of every future difficulty. If international relations could be worse strained under Technocracy than they are today, Technocracy would, indeed, work wonders.

What to do about foreign debts would be a problem, indeed. But so it is today. The enormous amount of domestic debt has piled up a problem of such immediate agony that it seems to be insoluble, except by the process of elimination by avalanche, default, bankruptcy, and the annihilation going on so furiously the last few years. It should not be hard to find a way to make a fair exchange from old values to new.

Technocracy is a plan to bring order into the present chaos and construct a decent workaday world.

This article was written in *Liberty Magazine*
February 18, 1933

Web: www.technocracyinc.org

(ISSN 154-2797) Regular Price $2.00
Third Quarter, 2003
Issue No. 5, vol. 2
Ferndale, WA 98248-9764

OUR FALTERING PLANET

Mother Earth Needs a Rest

As we go through our daily lives working, playing, loving, and sometimes hating, we get so mired in the things we feel are so important that we lose all connections with the systems that make all these "important" things possible. We lose more than just connections—we lose the assurance that the next generations will even have a chance to do what we take for granted.

We should not be so critical of ourselves though, because no matter how cognizant we become, no matter our intelligence quotient, without proper direction and commitment from our nation's leadership, we have no chance of understanding the need for connecting to the greater scheme of things. The greater scheme of course, is our home, planet Earth.

Every day in the international press and a few of our major news sources, there are articles and programs on the escalating inability of our planet to regenerate its environmental systems. Two recent examples are in our local newspaper: the June 5th, 2003, Seattle Post-Intelligencer title d "America's oceans in crises," and also in the national publication of the US News and World Report in the June 9th, 2003, edition called "Empty Oceans: Why the World's Seafood

Supply Is Disappearing." At least in the work of a few concerned reporters, we do get examples of a connection. In some respects it is a mazing that we do get that much, because in North America the business ownership of most of our sources of "news" do not want the idea of business enterprise to be at fault with any of the problems we face today. More insidious is the fact that our leadership is now controlled by campaign contributions and bribes of these same businesses and their associates, so that we become subjected to more and more diversions, exclusions and outright lies.

Instead of pointing fingers and playing the "blame game," it is more constructive to try to analyze the reasons for conducting policy in this manner. Economics is a high-stakes game of winners and losers and so much is dependent on winning the game by establishing confidence in the game itself. The big players—corporations, businesses, financial enterprises, and unions—are instrumental in striving to maintain the system for their benefit. But we really cannot fault them either, for they are playing the game or using the system as it was designed. The real challenge set before us is the ability to recognize that we must implement a new game. Not just because it would be more fair or just, but because it means our very survival. If our oceans fail us, then it will not be long before our lovely planet succumbs. And we will deserve our fate because we failed the earth.

We cannot end this without emphasizing that the most significant obstacle to local and global problems of all kinds is the unrelenting population growth in all areas of the world. Only a Technocratic functional system that is designed as a steady state, and does not require an exponential growth as our present Price System can possibly have any success at tackling this tremendous problem.

People-you must understand that we are not publishing this magazine for the fun of it. You absolutely have no future if you do not take a stand and scream for a change of direction before it is too late. We challenge you here and now to investigate Technocracy's design that can redirect our suicidal behavior. You only have the human race to save.

—Editor

www.technocracyinc.org

The North American Technocrat (ISSN 0029-3474) is published quarterly by The North American Technocrat Managing Board, Technocracy Inc., 2475 Harksell Road, Ferndale, WA 98248. Single copy $2.00. Year subscriptions: $6.00. Periodicals postage paid at Ferndale, WA, and additional mailing offices. POSTMASTER: Send address changes to *The North American Technocrat*, 2475 Harksell Road, Ferndale, WA 98248.

Americans . . .
Leading the Way . . . Destroying the Planet: What's the World to Do?

Published on Thursday, September 12, 2002, by CommonDreams.org
By Lynn Landes

It wasn't enough for George Bush to boycott the Earth Summit. He sent negotiators flanked by big business to Johannesburg to destroy it. And Bush had other help as well. He had lots of support from ordinary folks back home. Average Americans are destroying the planet with their fossil-fuel lifestyle. And they don't seem to care how it affects the world around them.

The tiny island of Tuvalu in the South Pacific has given up hope. It's evacuating its population of fourteen thousand to New Zealand. The sixteen-square-mile island is sinking into the ocean due to rising sea levels caused by global warming. The world is under assault by catastrophic floods, fires, and droughts. And most people are blaming the United States.

Oh sure, other countries also contribute to climate change. But given that the US is responsible for 25 percent to the world's carbon dioxide emissions while representing only 4.6 percent of the population-we are clearly leading the way. Although it's common practice to place all the blame at the feet of America's corrupt corporations and spineless politicians, that becomes increasingly difficult when SUVs now account for 23 percent of all new car sales nationwide and 47 percent in California alone.

So what's the world to do? How can foreign peoples and their governments make an impression on apathetic Americans? More talks?

More summits? Not now. The Earth just showed how easily it can be sabotaged. Short of violence, which is commonly used for good and ill by American presidents both past and present, foreign governments and individuals could expand on a three-part strategy already in limited use-sue, boycott, and get "personal" with Americans.

Let's start in reverse order. First, get personal-man to man. Let Americans you meet hear your outrage. Violate our comfort zone. You're not asking for less consumerism from Americans, just clean and green rather than coal and oil, or at least cars that get over twenty miles per gallon, for Pete's sake. Many countries are forging ahead with substantial wind, solar, and fuel-cell projects, while George Bush promotes coal, oil, and nuclear energy. And Americans let him get away with that.

Next, boycott American goods and services. Don't prop up our economy with your investments and consumer spending. Already there's a fairly successful boycott in many parts of the world against (mostly US) genetically modified crops. And boycotts certainly worked to liberate South Africa from apartheid. Capitalism responds when businesses take a hit.

And, for the final and third strategy, foreign nations and individuals can sue America. There's growing interest in international environmental litigation. And the island of Tuvalu may lead the way. It's considering lawsuits against the United States and Australia for refusing to ratify the 1997 Kyoto protocol on cutting greenhouse gas emissions to prevent global warming.

For the first time, Americans are suing our own institutions for causing global warming. Friends of the Earth, Greenpeace, and the city of Boulder, Colorado, filed the suit against the Export-Import Bank (Ex-Im) and the Overseas Private Investment Corporation (OPIC), alleging that these taxpayer-funded lending institutions illegally provided more than $32 billion in financing and insurance for oil fields, pipelines, and coal-fired power plants without assessing their contribution to global warming and their impact on the US environment as required under key provisions of the National Environmental Policy Act (NEPA). It's about time.

International environmental law was the focus of a meeting of more than a hundred judges and lawyers at the Earth Summit in Johannesburg. The "Johannesburg Principles on the Role of Law and Sustainable Development" were adopted at the Global Judges Symposium organized by the United Nations Environment Program (UNEP). It states, "the fragile state of the global environment requires the Judiciary, as the guardian of the Rule of Law, to boldly and fearlessly implement and enforce applicable international and national laws . . ." Nice words and it's a start, but without US support, the Johannesburg Principles will certainly have rough going.

Americans live in geographic and cultural isolation. Getting their attention is a tough assignment. Getting them tuned in to saving the planet may be even tougher. But the time for politeness is over. People and nations around the world are in a battle of survival largely because of American reliance on fossil fuels. And if foreign countries and their people have to get in our face, or boycott our businesses, or sue us in order to save themselves, then so be it.

If these strategies don't work, the case for violence will be made. For the peoples of the world, protecting the environment is a question of life and death, not comfort or convenience.

Lynn Landes is a freelance journalist specializing in environmental issues. She writes a weekly column which is published on her website www.EcoTalk.org and reports environmental news for DUTV in Philadelphia, PA. Lynn s been a radio show host and a regular commentator for a BBG radio program

Planet's Future at Stake, UN Report Says

Published on Thursday, May 23, 2002 in the *Toronto Star*

> "It would be a disaster to sit back and ignore the picture that is painted."
>
> Klaus Toepfer, UN Environment
> Program by Olivia Ward

LONDON—In thirty years, the Earth could look like a desert-strewn wasteland of urban slums, lose almost a quarter of its mammal species, and leave people inhabiting large regions perishing from thirst and water-borne disease.

Or, it could be stabilizing global warming, repairing damage to water resources and the worst effects of environmentally induced poverty.

According to a massive United Nations environmental study released yesterday, the planet is poised on a precipice, and time is running out for making tough political and economic choices that can pull it back from disaster.

"The choices made today are critical for the forests, oceans, rivers, mountains, and other life-support systems upon which current and future generations depend," said Klaus Toepfer, executive director of the UN Environment Program (UNEP), based in Nairobi, Kenya.

"Fundamental changes are possible and required," he added. "It would be a disaster to sit back and ignore the picture that is painted."

Home Foreclosures at Thirty-Year High

By Thomas A. Fogarty, *USA Today*
09/09 /2002

A record percentage of US homeowners are facing foreclosure, and many more are falling behind on monthly house payments.

"During April, May and June, 1.23% of mortgages—about 640,000—were in the foreclosure process. That's the highest rate in its 30 years of tracking," the Mortgage Bankers Association said Monday. "A year earlier, not even 1% of mortgages were in foreclosure."

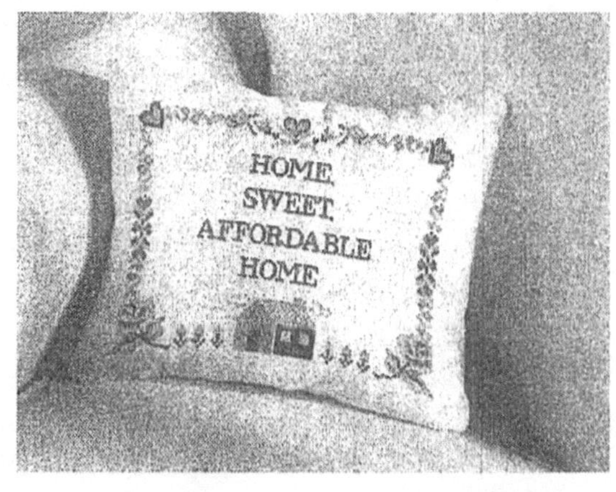

"Though the inclination might be to blame the economy, it's more than that," industry observers say. "Other factors might be at work."

Changes in the way lending is done, for example, could help explain the trend. The past decade has brought a proliferation in mortgage products-including interest-only and low-down-payment loans. "Many of these products are being stress-tested for the first time in a recession," MBA chief eco nom is t Doug Duncan says.

"The high level of foreclosures is surprising for two reasons," Duncan says, "Economic conditions aren't all that dire, and previous surveys hadn't been showing a level of delinquencies that would predict record foreclosures."

John Karevoll, a DataQuick analyst who independently has tracked an uptick in foreclosures, says it might reflect greater willingness by lenders to use foreclosure to compel payment. "I'm told they're starting to use the foreclosure process to crack the whip a little more than they once did," Karevoll said. "Housing remains strong in most markets," he says, "giving the borrower or lender opportunity for a quick resale at a good price."

Other likely culprits:

- The job market. "Unemployment averaged 5.9% in the April–June quarter, a recent high. Homeowners out of work find it harder to make payments, because the job market will likely remain soft," Duncan says, "the proportion of borrowers under stress might stay high for six months or so."
- Social policy. Government efforts to broaden home ownership have resulted in nearly 68% of Americans owning homes, a record. But the efforts also have meant lending to higher-risk borrowers.
- Consumer debt. As millions have refinanced, many have rolled high-interest consumer debt into their mortgages. "Doing so puts the house at risk when times get tight. Some distressed borrowers have been able to sidestep foreclosure by refinancing to lower interest rates and cutting monthly payments," Duncan said.

In addition to high overall numbers of borrowers in foreclosure, the quarter also saw the highest percentage against whom foreclosure was initiated—0.4%. The MBA survey also recorded an increase in homeowners more than 30 days behind in scheduled house payments, but not yet far enough behind to face foreclosure. On a seasonally adjusted basis, 4.77% of mortgage borrowers were delinquent in the April–June quarter, vs. 4.65% the previous quarter. The delinquency rate remains below records of the mid-1980s, when it ran 6%-plus.

Our Crushing Personal Debt

By David S. Broder
Sunday, September 1, 2002

As usual, the Labor Day weekend has found politicians of both parties bragging about their devotion to working families. The emphasis is not misplaced, but the substance of their speeches is often suspect.

He re, for example, is a startling statement you are not likely to hear from anyone seeking office: "For the typical house hold, rising debt, not a rising stock market, was the big story of the 1990s. House hold debt grew much more rapidly than house hold income in the last decade."

I did not know that, and my hunch is that you may not have been aware of it either. It is one of the thousands of facts embedded in a volume called "The State of Working America," a biennial report by three economists at the Economic Policy Institute in Washington.

The institute is a labor-funded think tank, and that sponsorship is reflected in some of the analysis. But Lawrence Mishel, its president, and co-authors Jared Bernstein and Heather Boushey buttress their arguments with data from the Census Bureau, the Federal Reserve Board and other establishment sources. And their emphasis on middle-class families is a welcome respite from all the stories about the ruin of corporate executives and the damage to people's 401 (k) plans.

So much has been written about this becoming "a nation of stockholders" that the Dow Jones average has turned into the most popular index of Americans' well-being. It is important, but, as this study reminds us, jobs and wages and income are a lot more vital to most people than the state of their stock portfolios.

Peril at the Crossroads

The Application of Intelligent Thought

What technocracy has said for almost eighty years is that the continued application of science and technology to our price system will destroy it.

Scientists are warning that we have only one or two generations to avoid global catastrophe. Why aren't we heeding their warnings, and what can be done?

These warnings have appeared in many forms and forums. "The Club of Rome Report" was recently discussed on the Energy Resources site. Why are warnings no heeded? Well, when you live in a society where money talks and monetary wealth is in control, expect no changes that will upset the apple cart. The world moves via various currencies, money.

All governments in the world are price systems.

It is important to understand that technocracy has no quarrel with the operation of the price system other than it is incapable of operating a high-energy system in a rational manner that would preclude a devastating end result from its continued operation. A price system operates quite well in small-scale agrarian communities such as those where it was first developed. A price system also works quite well when there exist substitutes for whatever is being sold. It automatically adjusts for shortages and plentiful supplies.

There are many who decry and condemn technology for our current problems. While it is true that we would not have developed our current level of resource consumption, and therefore depletion without the development of technology, technology is inanimate. It is not capable of doing anything. It is we who are doing it, using that technology. The reason we are doing those things is because of our social organization-a price system. To blame technology for the faults of society is rather like blaming a wastepaper basket for the existence of waste paper. What technocracy has said for almost eighty years is that the continued application of science and technology to our price system will destroy it. Currently there seems to be a race between whether we or our resources will be exhausted first. One thing that is far from having been exhausted is the application of intelligent thought.

A price system needs several things to keep it working properly. As anyone working in agriculture knows, scarcity creates value. If something is not scarce, value disappears. A price system needs jobs to distribute income. The consequence of applying technology is to eliminate both.

It is obvious, to anyone who cares to look with some insight and detail into our current situation, that all resources need to be conserved to the maximum. It is quite clear that without substantial reduction of human population there is little chance for even the cleverest technology to have any positive effect. One has only to look at any of the most popular media to see that this subject is not even on the radar screen today. The largest contributor to US population growth is immigration. Business likes a steady supply of cheap labor, which immigration supplies. Probably the saddest condition is that many of the environmental organizations have bought into the idea that objection to continued immigration is tantamount to racism.

Technocracy has always promoted projects that were intended to improve the energy efficiency of North America. Examination of some projects which would achieve that end, and the most likely response of the price system are instructive. It is quite obvious that travel by air is expensive in terms of energy. Rail travel is far more conservative for travel but is unpopular here because it is so slow and uncertain. The large railroad companies want nothing to do with it and would probably be much happier if it just went away.

A recent article in *Mechanical Engineering* magazine stated that the construction of a magnetically levitated rail system would take approximately 5,000 tons of steel per mile. My own calculations show that, using 133-lb. rail, 234 tons per mile would be required for a two rail standard system. However, that figure does not count structural steel requirements. Passenger trains currently have to share rail with freight, which has right of way. A completely separate passenger line should be constructed on which only passenger trains would be allowed. It should be constructed so that there are no crossings. It should be designed for travel at 200 mph or better. Such a system, especially given some governmental support, could replace much air travel, a far higher efficiency thereby displacing much imported fuel. As fuel availability declines, such luxuries as air travel will become increasingly rare. A high-speed rail system could keep North America united by maintaining the possibility of travel continent wide.

This seems like a reasonable response to a problem until one considers what the response of the airline industry, the automobile industry, and numerous others might very well be to such a proposal. Why would a large negative response be anticipated? Would the objections be on the grounds of engineering feasibility? As there are several such systems in current successful use, that seems unlikely. When any large bureaucracy then, whether private or governmental, is in place, it will act in a manner to maintain its position whether there is any sense to it or not. It will do so in order to maintain its income.

It is also quite apparent that any improvement in fuel economy of passenger vehicles would be a great help in reduction of the usage of petroleum resources. It seems scarcely necessary to mention the response to this sort of thinking. Even with the technology available to produce respectable results, there is no interest in using it. Only profitability matters. The effect of what is being produced for society, whether beneficial or harmful, means nothing.

The construction of a pipe-type electrical transmission line of a million volts DC with a carrying capacity of about 20,000 MW interconnecting the North American Continent both north to south and east to west would be a good, if somewhat expensive, idea. It would permit the elimination of the most inefficient generators as well as making it possible to transmit renewable energy from the many places where it is not needed to those where it is. By putting the cable in concrete raceways next to major highways, access roads would not be needed. Much of the present 500 KV overhead lines could probably be eliminated, thereby reducing the need for maintenance.

The reception of such a suggestion is likely to be rather cold unless some major corporation became convinced that a lot of money could be made from it. If a new idea was not invented by a particular corporation, with the support of the management, there is little chance of it being adopted or even seriously investigated. Ideas that come from the inside of a corporation or organization are likely to support the structure of that organization. An organization or a particular technology develops a constituency. Those who work in the organization or technology understand it and feel threatened by any outside pressures. The threat is financial, in other words, a price-system organization, whether private or public, acts in such a manner as to maintain its own existence. Any new idea is likely to be attacked as unworkable or impractical if it is acknowledged at all.

In a price system, costs are usually reduced by improving the technology used in production. Over the last decade cost were reduced by moving much of the most labor-intensive industries to areas where labor was cheaper. As the cost of transportation increases, much of that industry will begin to move closer to the markets they serve. At that point, one can expect dramatic improvements in productivity in the form of near-total automation of production and management functions. Several conditions are necessary for proper functioning of a price system. Price itself cannot be maintained without a scarcity. This was most clearly demonstrated during the depression of the 1930s with farmers plowing their crops under to maintain a scarcity. A price system distributes its purchasing power through jobs. If there are none, or simply too few, the system cannot be maintained. A price system needs continuous growth. Contraction leads to collapse. I would urge those interested in investigating this further to read Jeremy Rifkin's book *The End of Work* troubled by the fact that "news" stories like the Jessica Lynch rescue tale are now revealed (by our closest ally and even by our own corporate press) to be nothing but manufactured lies. You still have difficulty overlooking your government's multiple violations of international law, resulting in the deaths of thousands of innocent civilians. Or perhaps the fruitless search for the all-important but apparently nonexistent Weapons of mass destruction has gotten you down.

If you, like millions of others, still suffer from anxiety over these troubling events, the time has come to take decisive action. You can put all such worries out of your mind once and for all. At long last, there is an affordable new treatment that utilizes the best elements of medical science, psychology, and corporate-engineered mind control. Now you can achieve guaranteed, permanent results, with very little effort, and minimal expense. Now, you too can have your very own frontal lobotomy!

I can already hear you skeptics out there, with questions such as the following: Haven't lobotomies been around for decades? What's so fresh and new about this idea? Isn't brain surgery a bit extreme? Since I already watch Fox News and read the *New York Times*, why would I need a lobotomy? Wouldn't it be redundant? Read on, silent sufferers, because this is the only product on the market today with the power to put your mind completely at ease. Don't allow your fear to stand in the way of its cure. The lobotomy has been around for a number of years, but its therapeutic potential has been limited by a reluctance on the part of practitioners to expand its use to treat common anxiety. But our cutting-edge research indicates that eliminating the area of the brain that carries out analytical functions is the only foolproof way to eradicate the cognitive dissonance caused by awareness of the huge discrepancy between reality and progovernment corporate propaganda.

Think about it. If you no longer have the capacity for rational thought, no longer have the ability to discern fact from fiction, you will be free to live a hassle-free, happy life. You will be unconcerned with the annoying and petty details of life, free from the burden of having to distinguish between right and wrong. Only then can you be truly free to wholeheartedly support unspeakable atrocities committed by your government and paid for with your tax dollars.

Sure, corporate media is doing its part to exclude any mention of stories that might disturb your peace of mind. And in the wake of the recent FCC decision to allow further media consolidation in the hands of ultra-right-wing billionaires, like Rupert Murdoch, you can expect even more disturbing news to disappear from the headlines. But can you really expect corporate media to do the whole job?

We maintain that it is too much to ask that government and corporate manipulation of information provide you with all of the relief you seek. For insight into why this is true, you have only to look at a few of the basic assumptions that they must sell you before you can feel good about your government. Just look at this partial list:

A. Waging unprovoked, preemptive war will preserve peace.
B. The world will be a safer place after America embarks on an expensive new arms buildup, constructs new nuclear weapons, attacks sovereign foreign nations at will, and demands that all those same nations that we are attacking, threatening, and arming ourselves against, must immediately disarm.
C. Massive tax cuts for billionaires in a time of ballooning deficits, while teachers are being laid off nationwide and social services are being slashed, will be good for average Americans. The extra cash available to people with multi-million-dollar annual salaries will be just the money that inspires these billionaires to start new businesses. The incredibly large and ever-expanding, gap between rich and poor has left the super rich perpetually just one massive tax cut below the threshold at which they will suddenly be inspired to invest in an all-out effort to provide jobs for unemployed Americans.
D. Providing Israel with billions of dollars' worth of weaponry every year and looking the other way while the Israeli

government seizes Palestinian land, destroys homes, and kills civilians, is an essential and helpful part of the Peace Process.

E. Concentration of media ownership in the hands of a few billionaires will lead to diversity of programming. The concept is succinctly expressed by this equation: Monopoly equals diversity.

F. Obvious lies are not lies, because you can trust us to be balanced and fair.

G. Pay no attention to the man behind the curtain.

In the 1930s, Howard Scott stated that the application of technology and energy to the price system would result in its destruction. This has not occurred as fast as most Technocrats thought or would have liked, but the trends continue. The normal response to this situation is to try to stop the technology from moving in that direction. The response of Technocracy was that if the Price System is going to collapse, why not design a society that would operate on some other basis than that of money?

A society as large and complex as ours still needs the type of feedback controls that money provides. Energy is the most fundamental constituent of anything physical and is the most logical thing to use as a measurement and control variable. The measurement of energy in any industrial process is not generally very difficult. It is simply not usually done by price systems unless one is being charged directly for its use.

A society that operates on a non-price basis would be as different in structure and culture as our society today is from that of the Roman Empire or that of the ancient Egyptians. Money is both the mechanism and the motivation for the control of people and society. Those who possess it want to keep those who don't from getting what they have. If one examines the society we have today, it become evident that the vast majority of what is today described as our social system consists of laws to protect property. Successful wealth accumulation by lying, cheating, or outright theft is built into every Price System. Ever-new swindles generate an endless progression of new law. The People's Congress has aided and continues to aid those most able to assist them in keeping their powerful positions. "You scratch my back, I'll scratch yours," the general public's welfare be damned!

From the archives of Technocracy Inc.

Credit: Ron Miller

www.technocracyinc.org

From Edward Bellamy's *Looking Backward*, 1888

Assumption by government of the charge of the national industries. We should have thought that no arrangement could be worse than to entrust the politicians with control of the wealth-producing machinery of the country. Its material interests were quite too much the football of parties as it was."

"No doubt you were right," rejoined Doctor Leete, "but all that is changed now. We have no parties or politicians, and as for demagoguery and corruption, they are words having only an historical significance."

"Human nature itself must have changed very much," I said.

"Not at all," was Doctor Leete's reply, "but the conditions of human life have changed, and with them the motives of human action. The organization of society with you was such that officials were under a constant temptation to misuse their power for the private profit of themselves or others. Under such circumstances it seems almost strange that you dared entrust them with any of your affairs. Nowadays, on the contrary, society is so constituted that there is absolutely no way in which an official, however ill-disposed, could possibly make any profit for himself or any one else by a misuse of his power. Let him be as bad an official as you please, he cannot be a corrupt one. There is no motive to be. The social system no longer offers a premium on dishonesty. But these are matters which you can only understand as you come, with time, to know us better."

"But you have not yet told me how you have settled the labor problem. It is the problem of capital which we have been discussing," I said. "After the nation had assumed conduct of the mills, machinery, railroads, farms, mines, and capital in general of the country, the labor question still remained. In assuming the responsibilities of capital the nation had assumed the difficulties of the capitalist's position."

"The moment the nation assumed the responsibilities of capital those difficulties vanished," replied Doctor Leete. "The national organization of labor under one direction was the complete solution of what was, in your day and under your system, justly regarded as the insoluble labor problem. When the nation became the sole employer, all the citizens, by virtue of their citizenship, became employees, to be distributed according to the needs of industry."

"That is," I suggested, "you have simply applied the principle of universal military service, as it was understood in our day, to the labor question."

"Yes," said Doctor Leete, "that was something which followed as a matter of course as soon as the nation had become the sole capitalist. The people were already accustomed to the idea that the obligation of every citizen, not physically disabled, to contribute his military services to the defense of the nation was equal and absolute. That it was equally the duty of every citizen to contribute his quota of industrial or intellectual services to the maintenance of the nation was equally evident, though it was not until the nation became the employer of labor that citizens were able to render this sort of service with any pretense either of universality or equity. No organization of labor was possible when the employing power was divided among hundreds or thousands of individuals and corporations, between which concert of any kind was neither desired, nor indeed feasible. It constantly happened then that vast numbers who desired to labor could find no opportunity, and on the other hand, those who desired to evade a part or all of their debt could easily do so."

"Service, now, I suppose, is compulsory upon all," I suggested.

"It is rather a matter of course than compulsion," replied Doctor Leete. "It is regarded as so absolutely natural and reasonable that the idea of its being compulsory has ceased to be thought of. He would be thought to be an incredibly contemptible person who should need compulsion in such a case. Nevertheless, to speak of service being compulsory would be a weak way to state its absolute inevitableness. Our entire social order is so wholly based upon and deduced from it that if it were conceivable that a man could escape it, he would be left with no possible way to provide for his existence. He would have excluded himself from the world, cut himself off from his kind, in a word, committed suicide."

"Is the term of service in this industry army for life?"

"Oh, no; it both begins later and ends earlier than the average working period in your day. Your workshops were filled with children and old men, but we hold the period of youth sacred to education, and the period of maturity, when the physical forces begin to flag, equally sacred to ease and agreeable relaxation. The period of industrial service is twenty-four years, beginning at the close of the course of education at twenty-one and terminating at forty-five. After forty-five, while discharged from labor, the citizen still remains liable to special calls, in case of emergencies causing a sudden great increase in the demand for labor, till he reaches the age of fifty-five, but such calls are rarely, in fact almost never, made. The fifteenth day of October of every year is what we call Muster Day, because those who have reached the age of twenty-one are then mustered into the industrial service, and at the same time those who, after twenty-four years' service, have reached the age of forty-five are honorably mustered out. It is the great day of the year with us, whence we reckon all other events, our Olympiad, save that it is annual."

<h2 style="text-align:center">•VII•</h2>

"It is after you have mustered your industrial army into service," I said, "that I should expect the difficulty to arise, for there its analogy with a military army must cease. Soldiers have all the same thing, and a very simple thing, to do, namely, to practice the manual of arms, to march and stand guard. But the industrial army must learn and follow two or three hundred diverse trades and avocations. What administrative talent can be equal to determine wisely what trade or business every individual in a great nation shall pursue?"

"The administration has nothing to do with determining that point." "Who does determine it, then?" I asked.

"Every man for himself in accordance with his natural aptitude, the utmost pains being taken to enable him to find out what his natural aptitude really is. The principle on which our industrial army is organized is that a man's natural endowments, mental and physical, determine what he can work at most profitably to the nation and most satisfactorily to himself. While the obligation of service in some form is not to be evaded, voluntary election, subject only to necessary regulation, is depended on to determine the particular sort of service every man is to render. As an individual's satisfaction during his term of service depends on his having an occupation to his taste, parents and teachers watch from early years for indications of special aptitudes in children. A thorough study of the national industrial system, with the history and rudiments of all the great trades, is an essential part of our education system. While manual training is not allowed to encroach on the general intellectual culture to which our schools are devoted, it is carried far enough to give our youth, in addition to their theoretical knowledge of the national industries, mechanical and agricultural, a certain familiarity with their tools and methods. Our schools are constantly visiting our workshops, and often are taken on long excursions to inspect particular industrial enterprises. In your day a man was not ashamed to be grossly ignorant of all trades except his own, but such ignorance would not be consistent with our idea of placing every one in a position to select intelligently the occupation for which he has most taste. Usually long before he is mustered into service a young man has found out the pursuit he wants to follow, has acquired a great deal of knowledge about it, and is waiting impatiently the time when he can enlist in its ranks."

"Surely," I said, "it can hardly be that the number of volunteers for any trade is exactly the number needed in that trade. It must be generally either under or over in demand."

"Why, naturally," I said, "inasmuch as they are incapable of self-support."

But here the doctor took me up quickly.

"Who is capable of self-support?" he demanded. "There is no such thing in a civilized society as self-support. In a state of society so barbarous as not even to know family cooperation, each individual may possibly support himself, though even then for a part of his life only; but from the moment that men begin to live together, and constitute even the rudest of society, self-support becomes impossible. As men grow more civilized, and the subdivision of occupations and services is carried out, a complex mutual dependence becomes the universal rule. Every man, however solitary may seem his occupation, is a member of a vast industrial partnership, as large as the nation, as large as humanity. The necessity of mutual dependence should imply the duty and guarantee of mutual support; and that it did not in your day constituted the essential cruelty and unreason of your system."

"That may all be so," I replied, "but it does not touch the case of those who are unable to contribute anything to the product of industry." "Surely I told you this morning, at least I thought I did," replied Doctor Leete, "that the right of a man to maintenance at the nation's table depends on the fact that he is a man, and not on the amount of health and strength he may have, so long as he does his best."

"You said so," I answered, "but I supposed the rule applied only to the workers of different ability. Does it also hold of those who can do nothing at all?"

"Are they not also men?"

"I am to understand, then, that the lame, the blind, the sick, and the impotent, are as well off as the most efficient, and have the same income?"

"Certainly," was the reply.

"The idea of charity on such a scale," I answered, "would have made our most enthusiastic philanthropists gasp."

"If you had a sick brother at home," replied Doctor Leete, "unable to work, would you feed him on less dainty food, and lodge and clothe him more poorly, than yourself? More likely far, you would give him the preference; nor would you think of calling it charity. Would not the word, in that connection, fill you with indignation?"

"Of course," I replied, "but the cases are not parallel. There is a sense, no doubt, in which all men are brothers; but this general sort of brotherhood is not to be compared, except for rhetorical purposes, to the brotherhood of blood, either as to its sentiment or its obligations."

Chunks Gods World

"There speaks the nineteenth century!" exclaimed Doctor Leete. "Ah, Mr. West, there is no doubt as to the length of time that you slept. If I were to give you, in one sentence, a key to what may seem the mysteries of our civilization as compared with that of your age, I should say that it is the fact that the solidarity of the race and the brotherhood of man, which to you were but fine phrases, are, to our thinking and feeling, ties as real and as vital as physical fraternity.

"But even setting that consideration aside, I do not see why it so surprises you that those who cannot work are conceded the full right to live on the produce of those who can. Even in your day the duty of military service for the protection of the nation, to which our industrial service corresponds, while obligatory on those able to discharge it, did not operate to deprive of the privileges of citizenship those who were unable. They stayed at home, and were protected by those who fought, and nobody questioned their right to be, or thought less of them. So, now, the requirement of industrial service from those able to render it does not operate to deprive of the privileges of citizenship, which now implies the citizen's maintenance, him who cannot work. The worker is not a citizen because he works, but works because he is a citizen. As you recognize the duty of the strong to fight for the weak, we, now that fighting is gone by, recognize his duty to work for him.

"A solution which leaves an unaccounted—for residuum is no solution at all; and our solution of the problem of human society would have been none at all had it left the lame, the sick, and the blind outside with the beasts, to fare as they might. Better far have left the strong and well unprovided for than these burdened ones, toward whom every heart must yearn, and for whom ease of mind and body should be provided, if for no others. Therefore it is, as I told you this morning, that the title of every man, woman, and child to the means of existence rests on no basis less plain, broad, and simple than the fact that they are fellows of one race-members of one human family. The only coin current is the image of God, and that is good for all we have.

"I think there is no feature of the civilization of your epoch so repugnant to modem ideas as the neglect with which you treated your dependent classes. Even if you had no pity, no feeling of brotherhood, how was it that you did not see that you were robbing the incapable class of their plain right in leaving them unprovided for?"

"I don't quite follow you there," I said. "I admit the claim of this class to our pity, but how could they who produced nothing claim a share of the product as a right?"

"How happened it," was Doctor Leete's reply, "that your workers were able to produce more than so many savages would have done? Was it not wholly on account of the heritage of the past knowledge and achievements of the race, the machinery of society, thousands of years in contriving, found by you ready-made to your hand? How did you come to be possessors of this knowledge and this machinery, which represent nine parts to one contributed by yourself in the value of your product? You inherited it, did you not? And were not these others, these unfortunate and crippled brothers whom you cast out, joint inheritors, coheirs with you? What did you do with their share? Did you not rob them when you put them off with crusts, who were entitled to sit with the heirs, and did you not add insult to robbery when you called the crusts charity?

"Ah, Mr. West," Doctor Leete continued, as I did not respond, "what I do not understand is, setting aside all considerations either of justice or brotherly feeling toward the crippled and defective, how the workers of your day could have had any heart for their work, knowing that their children, or grandchildren, if unfortunate, would be deprived of the comforts and even necessities of life. It is a mystery how men with children could favor a system under which they were rewarded beyond those less endowed with bodily strength or mental power. For, by the same discrimination by which the father profited, the son, for whom he would give his life, being perchance weaker than others, might be reduced to crusts and beggary. How men dared leave children behind them, I have never been able to understand."
note. Although in his talk on the previous evening Doctor Leete had emphasized the pains taken to enable every man to ascertain and follow his natural bent in choosing an occupation, it was not till I learned that the worker's income is the same in all occupations that I realized how absolutely he may be counted on to do so, and thus, by selecting the harness which sets most lightly on himself, find that

in which he can pull best. The failure of my age in any systematic or effective way to develop and utilize the natural aptitudes of men for the industries and intellectual avocations was one of the great wastes, as well as one of the most common causes of unhappiness in that time. The vast majority of my contemporaries, though nominally free to do so, never really chose their occupations at all, but were forced by circumstances into work for which they were relatively inefficient, because not naturally fitted for it. The rich, in this respect, had little advantage over the poor. The latter, indeed, being generally deprived of education, had no opportunity even to ascertain the natural aptitudes they might have, and on account of their poverty were unable to develop them by cultivation even when ascertained. The liberal and technical professions, except by favorable accident, were shut to them, to their own great loss and that of the nation. On the other hand, the well-to-do, although they could command education and opportunity, were scarcely less hampered by social prejudice, which forbade them to pursue manual avocations, even when adapted to them, and destined them, whether fit or unfit, to the professions, thus wasting many an excellent handi-paintings for the public buildings, and their favorable verdict carries with it the artist's remission from other tasks to devote himself to his vocation. On copies of his work disposed of, he also derives the same advantage as the author on sales of his books. In all these lines of original genius the plan pursued is the same-to offer a free field to aspirants, and as soon as exceptional talent is recognized, to release it from all trammels and let it have free course. The remission of other service in these cases is not intended as a gift or reward, but as the means of obtaining more and higher service. Of course there are various literary, art, and scientific institutes to which membership comes to the famous and is greatly prized. The highest of all honors in the nation, higher than the presidency, which calls merely for good sense and devotion to duty, is the red ribbon awarded by the vote of the people to the great authors, artists, engineers, physicians, and inventors of the generation. Not over a certain number wear it at any one time, though every bright young fellow in the country loses innumerable nights' sleep dreaming of it. I even did myself."

"Just as if Mamma and I would have thought any more of you with it," exclaimed Edith, "not that it isn't, of course, a very fine thing to have."

"You have no choice, my dear, but to take your father as you found him and make the best of him," Doctor Leete replied. "But as for your mother, there, she would never have had me if I had not assured her that I was bound to get the red ribbon or at least the blue."

On this extravagance Mrs. Leete's only comment was a smile. "How about periodicals and newspapers?" I said. "I won't deny

that your book-publishing system is a considerable improvement on ours, both as to its tendency to encourage a real literary vocation, and, quite as important, to discourage mere scribblers; but I don't see how it can be made to apply to magazines and newspapers. It is very well to make a man pay for publishing a book, because the expense will be only occasional; but no man could afford the expense of publishing a newspaper every day in the year. It took the deep pockets of our private capitalists to do that, and often exhausted even them before the returns came in. If you have newspapers at all, they must, I fancy, be published by the government at the public expense, with government editors, reflecting government opinions. Now, if your system is so perfect that there is never anything to criticize in the conduct of affairs, this arrangement may answer. Otherwise I should think the lack of an independent unofficial medium for the expression of public opinion would have most unfortunate results. Confess, Doctor Leete, that a free newspaper press, with all that it implies, was a redeeming incident of the old system when capital was in private hands, and that you have to set off the loss of that against your gains in other respects."

"I am afraid I can't give you even that consolation," replied Doctor Leete, laughing. "In the first place, Mr. West, the newspaper press is by no means the only or, as we look at it, the best vehicle for serious criticism of public affairs. To us, the judgments of your newspapers on such themes seem generally to have been crude and flippant, as well as deeply tinctured with prejudice and bitterness. Insofar as they may be taken as expressing public opinion, they give an unfavorable impression of the popular intelligence, while so far as they may have formed public opinion, the nation was not to be felicitated. Nowadays, when a citizen desires to make a serious impression upon the public mind as to any aspect of public affairs, he comes out with a book or pamphlet, published as other books are. But this is not because we lack newspapers and magazines, or that they lack the most absolute freedom. The newspaper press is organized so as to be a more perfect expression of public opinion than it possibly could be in your day, when private capital controlled and managed it primarily as a money-making business, and secondarily only as a mouthpiece for the people."

"But," said I, "if the government prints the papers at the public expense, how can it fail to control their policy? Who appoints the editors, if not the government?"

"The government does not pay the expense of the papers, nor appoint their editors, nor in any way exert the slightest influence on their policy," replied Doctor Leete. "The people who take the paper pay the expense of its publication, choose its editor, and remove him when unsatisfactory. You will scarcely say, I think, that such a newspaper press is not a free organ of popular opinion."

"Decidedly I shall not," I replied, "but how is it practicable?" "Nothing could be simpler. Supposing some of my neighbors or myself think we ought to have a newspaper reflecting our opinions, and devoted especially to our locality, trade, or profession. We go about among the people till we get the names of such a number that their annual subscriptions will meet the cost of the paper, which is little or big according to the largeness of its constituency. The amount of the subscriptions marked off the credits of the citizens guarantees the nation against loss in publishing the paper, its business, you understand, being that of a publisher purely, with no option to refuse the duty required. The subscribers to the paper now elect somebody as editor, who, if he accepts the office, is discharged from other service during his incumbency. Instead of paying a salary to him, as in your day, the subscribers pay the nation an indemnity equal to the cost of his support for taking him away from the general service. He manages the paper just as one of your editors did, except that he has no counting room to obey, or interests of private capital as against the public good to defend. At the end of the first year, the subscribers for the next either re-elect the former editor or choose anyone else to his place. An able editor, of course, keeps his place indefinitely. As the subscription list enlarges, the funds of the paper increase, and it is improved by the securing of more and better contributors, just as your papers were."

"How is the staff of contributors recompensed, since they cannot be paid in money?"

"The editor settles with them the price of their wares. The amount is transferred to their individual credit from the guarantee credit of the paper, and a remission of service is granted the contributor for a length of time corresponding to the amount credited him, just as to other authors. As to magazines, the system is the same. Those interested in the prospectus of a new periodical pledge enough subscriptions to run it for a year; select their editor, who recompenses his contributors just as in the other case, the printing bureau furnishing the necessary force and material for publication, as a matter of course. When an editor's services are no longer desired, if he cannot earn the right to his time by other literary work, he simply resumes his place in the industrial army. I should add that, though ordinarily the editor is elected only at the end of the year, and as a rule is continued in office for a term of years, in case of any sudden change he should give to the tone of the paper, provision is made for taking the sense of the subscribers as to his removal at any time."

"However earnestly a man may long for leisure for purposes of study or meditation," I remarked, "he cannot get out of the harness, if I understand you rightly, except in these two ways you have mentioned. He must either by literary, artistic, or inventive productiveness indemnify the nation for the loss of his services, or must get a sufficient number of other people to contribute to such an indemnity."

"It is most certain," replied Doctor Leete, "that no able-bodied man nowadays can evade his share of work and live on the toil of others, whether he calls himself by the fine name of student or confesses to being simply lazy. At the same time our system is elastic enough to give free play to every instinct of human nature which does not aim at dominating others or living on the fruit of others' labor. There is not only the remission by indemnification but the remission by abnegation. Any man in his thirty-third year, his term of service being then half done, can obtain an honorable discharge from the army, provided he accepts for the rest of his life one-half the rate of maintenance other citizens receive. It is quite possible to live on this amount, though one must forego the luxuries and elegancies of life, with some, perhaps, of its comforts."

When the ladies retired that evening, Edith brought me a book and said:

"If you should be wakeful tonight, Mr. West, you might be interested in looking over this story by Berrian. It is considered his masterpiece, and will at least give you an idea what the stories nowadays are like."

I sat up in my room that night reading Penthesilia till it grew gray in the east, and did not lay it down till I had finished it. And yet let no admirer of the great romancer of the twentieth century resent my saying that at the first reading what most impressed me was not so much what was in the book as what was left out of it. The story writers of my day would have deemed the making of bricks without straw a light task compared with the construction of a romance from which should be excluded all effects drawn from the contrasts of wealth and poverty, education and ignorance, coarseness and refinement, high and low, all motives drawn from social pride and ambition, the desire of being richer or the fear of being poorer, together with sordid anxieties of any sort for one's self or others; a romance in which there should, indeed, be love galore, but love unfretted by artificial barriers created by differences of station or possessions, owning no other law but that of the heart. The reading of Penthesilia was of more value than almost any amount of explanation would have been in giving me something like a general impression of the social aspect of the twentieth century. The information Doctor Leete had imparted was indeed extensive as to facts, but they had affected my mind as so many separate impressions, which I had as yet succeeded but imperfectly in making cohere. Berrian put them together for me in a picture.

•XVI•

NEXT MORNING I ROSE SOMEWHAT BEFORE THE BREAKFAST hour. As I descended the stairs, Edith stepped into the hall from the room which had been the scene of the morning interview between us described some chapters back.

"Ah!" she exclaimed, with a charmingly arch expression, "you thought to slip out unbeknown for another of those solitary morning rambles which have such nice effects on you. But you see I am up too early for you this time. You are fairly caught."

"You discredit the efficacy of your own cure," I said, "by supposing that such a ramble would now be attended with bad consequences."

I FOUND THE PROCESSES AT THE WAREHOUSE QUITE as interesting as Edith had described them, and became even enthusiastic over the truly remarkable illustration which is seen there of the prodigiously multiplied efficiency which perfect organization can give to labor. It is like a gigantic mill, into the hopper of which goods are being constantly poured by the trainload and shipload, to issue at the other end in packages of pounds and ounces, yards and inches, pints and gallons, corresponding to the infinitely complex personal needs of half a million people. Doctor Leete, with the assistance of data furnished by me as to the way goods were sold in my day, figured out some astounding results in the way of the economies effected by the modern system.

As we set out homeward, I said: "After what I have seen today, together with what you have told me, and what I learned under Miss Leete's tutelage at the sample store, I have a tolerably clear idea of your system of distribution, and how it enables you to dispense with a circulating medium. But I should like very much to know something more about your system of production. You have told me in general how your industrial army is levied and organized, but who

214

directs its efforts? What supreme authority determines what shall be done in every department, so that enough of everything is produced and yet no labor wasted? It seems to me that this must be a wonderfully complex and difficult function, requiring very unusual endowments."

"Does it indeed seem so to you?" responded Doctor Leete. "I assure you that it is nothing of the kind, but on the other hand so simple, and depending on principles so obvious and easily applied, that the functionaries at Washington to whom it is trusted require to be nothing more than men of fair abilities to discharge it to the entire satisfaction of the nation. The machine which they direct is indeed a vast one, but so logical in its principles and direct and simple in its workings, that it all but runs itself; and nobody but a fool could derange it, as I think you will agree after a few words of explanation. Since you already have a pretty good idea of the working of the distributive system, let us begin at the_ end. Even in your day statisticians were able to tell you the number of yards of cotton, velvet, woolen, the number of barrels of flour, potatoes, butter, number of pairs of shoes, hats, and umbrellas annually consumed by the nation. Owing to the fact that production was in private hands, and that there was no way of getting statistics of actual distribution, these figures were not exact, but they were nearly so. Now that every pin which is given out from a national warehouse is recorded, of course the figures of consumption for any week, month, or year, in the possession of the department of distribution at the end of that period, are precise. On these figures, allowing for tendencies to increase or decrease and for any causes likely to affect demand, the estimates, say, for a year ahead, are based. These estimates, with a proper margin for security, having been accepted by the general administration, the responsibility of the distributive department ceases until the goods are delivered to it. I speak of the estimates being furnished for an entire year ahead, but in reality they cover that much time only in case of the great staples for which the demand can be calculated on as steady. In the great majority of smaller industries for the product of which popular taste fluctuates, and novelty is frequently required, production is kept barely ahead of consumption, the distributive department furnishing frequent estimates based on the weekly state of demand.

"Now the entire field of productive and constructive industry is divided into ten great departments, each representing a group of allied industries, each particular industry being in tum represented by a subordinate bureau, which has a complete record of the plant and force under its control, of the present product, and means of increasing it. The estimates of the distributive department, after adoption by the administration, are sent as mandates to the ten great departments, which allot them to the subordinate bureaus representing the particular industries, and these set the men at work. Each bureau is responsible for the task given it, and this responsibility is enforced by departmental oversight and that of the administration; nor does the distributive department accept the product without its own inspection; while even if in the hands of the consumer an article turns out unfit, the system enables the fault to be traced back to the original workman. The production of the commodities for actual public consumption does not, of course, require by any means all the national force of workers. After the necessary contingents have been detailed for the various industries, the amount of labor left for other employment is expended in creating fixed capital, such as buildings, machinery, engineering works, and so forth."

"One point occurs to me," I said, "on which I should think there might be dissatisfaction. Where there is no opportunity for private enterprise, how is there any assurance that the claims of small minorities of the people to have articles produced, for which there is no wide demand, will be respected? An official decree at any moment may deprive them of the means of gratifying some special taste, merely because the majority does not share it."

"That would be tyranny indeed," replied Doctor Leete, "and you may be very sure that it does not happen with us, to whom liberty is as dear as equality or fraternity. As you come to know our system better, you will see that our officials are in fact, and not merely in name, the agents and servants of the people. The administration has no power to stop the production of any commodity for which there continues to be a demand. Suppose the demand for any article declines to such a point that its production becomes very costly. The price has to be raised in proportion, of course, but as long as the consumer cares to pay it, the production goes on. Again, suppose an article not before produced is demanded. If the administration doubts that the reality of the demand, a popular petition guaranteeing a certain basis of consumption compels it to produce the desired article. A government, or a majority, which should undertake to tell the people, or a minority, what they were to eat, drink, or wear, as I believe governments in America did in your day, would be regarded as a curious anachronism indeed. Possibly you had reasons for tolerating these infringements of personal independence, but we should not think them endurable. I am glad you raised this point, for it has given me a chance to show you how much more direct and efficient is the control over production exercised by the individual citizen now than it was in your day, when what you called private initiative prevailed, though it should have been called capitalist initiative, for the average private citizen had little enough share in it."

"You speak of raising the price of costly articles," I said. "How can prices be regulated in a country where there is no competition between buyers or sellers?"

"Just as they were with you," replied Doctor Leete. "You think that needs explaining," he added, as I looked incredulous, "but the explanation need not be long; the cost of the labor which produced it was recognized as the legitimate basis of the price of an article in your day, and so it is in ours. In your day, it was the difference in wages that made the difference in the cost of labor; now it is the relative number of hours constituting a day's work in different trades, the maintenance of the worker being equal in all cases. The cost of a man's work in a trade so difficult that in order to attract volunteers the hours have to be fixed at four a day is twice as great as that in a trade where the men work eight hours. The result as to the cost of labor, you see, is just the same as if the man working four hours were paid, under your system, twice the wages the other gets. This calculation applied to the labor employed in the various processes of a manufactured article gives its price relatively to other articles. Besides the cost of production and transportation, the factor of scarcity affects the prices of some commodities. As regards the great staples of life, of which an abundance can always be secured, scarcity is eliminated as a factor. There is always a large surplus kept on hand from which any fluctuations of demand or supply can be corrected, even in most cases of bad crops. The prices of the staples grow less year by year, but rarely, if ever, rise. There are, however, certain classes of articles permanently, and others temporarily, unequal to the demand, as, for example, fresh fish or dairy products in the latter category, and the products of high skill and rare materials in the other. All that can be done here is to equalize the inconvenience of the scarcity. This is done by temporarily raising the price if the scarcity be temporary, or fixing it high if it be permanent. High prices in your day meant restriction of the articles affected to the rich, but nowadays, when the means of all are the same, the effect is only that those to whom the articles seem most desirable are the ones who purchase them. Of course the nation, as any other caterer for the public needs must be, is frequently left with small lots of goods on its hands by changes in taste, unseasonable weather, and various other causes. These it has to dispose of at a sacrifice just as merchants often did in your day, charging up the loss to the expenses of the business. Owing, however, to the vast body of consumers to which such lots can be simultaneously offered, there is rarely any difficulty in getting rid of them at trifling loss. I have given you now some general notion of our system of production, as well as distribution. Do you find it as complex as you expected?"

I admitted that nothing could be much simpler.

"I am sure," said Doctor Leete, "that it is within the truth to say that the head of one of the myriad private businesses of your day, who had to maintain sleepless vigilance against the fluctuations of the market, the machinations of his rivals, and the failure of his debtors, had a far more trying task than the group of men at Washington who nowadays direct the industries of the entire nation. All this merely shows, my dear fellow, how much easier it is to do things the right way than the wrong. It is easier for a general up in a balloon, with perfect survey of the field, to maneuver a million men to victory than for a sergeant to manage a platoon in a thicket."

"The general of this army, including the flower of the manhood of the nation, must be the foremost man in the country, really greater even than the President of the United States," I said.

"He is the President of the United States," replied Doctor Leete, "or rather the most important function of the presidency is the headship of the industrial army."

"How is he chosen?" I asked.

"I explained to you before," replied Doctor Leete, "when I was describing the force of the motive of emulation among all grades of the industrial army, that the line of promotion for the meritorious lies through three grades to the officer's grade, and thence up through the lieutenancies to the captaincy, or foremanship, and superintendency, or colonel's rank. Next, with an intervening grade in some of the larger trades, comes the general of the guild, under whose immediate control all the operations of the trade are conducted. This officer is at the head of the national bureau representing his trade, and is responsible for its work to the administration. The general of his guild holds a splendid position, and one which amply satisfies the ambition of most men, but above his rank, which may be compared—to follow the military analogies familiar to you—to that of a general of division, or major-general, is that of the chiefs of the ten great departments, or groups of allied trades. The chiefs of these ten grand divisions of the industrial army may be compared to your commanders of army corps, or lieutenant generals, each having from a dozen to a score of generals of separate guilds reporting to him. Above these ten great officers, who form his council, is the general-in-chief, who is the President of the United States.

"The general-in-chief of the industrial army must have passed through all the grades below him, from the common laborers up. Let us see how he rises. As I have told you, it is simply by the excellence of his record as a worker that one rises through the grades of the privates and becomes a candidate for a lieutenancy. Through the lieutenancies he rises to the colonelcy, or superintendent's position, by appointment from above, strictly limited to the candidates of the best records. The general of the guild appoints to the ranks under him, but he himself is not appointed, but chosen by suffrage."

"By suffrage!" I exclaimed. "Is not that ruinous to the discipline of the guild, by tempting the candidates to intrigue for the support of the workers under them?"

"So it would be, no doubt," replied Doctor Leete, "if the workers had any suffrage to exercise, or anything to say about the choice. But they have nothing. Just here comes in a peculiarity of our system. The general of the guild is chosen from among the superintendents by vote of the honorary members of the guild, that is, of those who have served their time in the guild and received their discharge. As you know, at the age of forty-five we are mustered out of the army of industry, and have the residue of life for the pursuit of our own improvement or recreation. Of course, however, the associations of our active lifetime retain a powerful hold on us. The companionships we formed then remain our companionships till the end of life. We always continue honorary members of our former guilds, and retain the keenest and most jealous interest in their welfare and repute in the hands of the following generation. In the clubs maintained by the honorary members of the several guilds, in which we meet socially, there are no topics of conversation so common as those which relate to these matters, and the young aspirants for guild leadership who can pass the criticism of us old fellows are likely to be pretty well equipped. Recognizing this fact, the nation entrusts to the honorary members of each guild the election of its general, and I venture to claim that no previous form of society could have developed a body of electors so ideally adapted to their office, as regards absolute impartiality, knowledge of the special qualifications and record of candidates, solicitude for the best result, and complete absence of self-interest.

"Each of the ten lieutenant generals, or heads of departments, is himself elected from among the generals of the guilds grouped as a department, by vote of the honorary members of the guilds thus grouped. Of course there is a tendency on the part of each guild to vote for its own general, but no guild of any group has nearly enough votes to elect a man not supported by most of the others. I assure you that these elections are exceedingly lively."

"The President, I suppose, is selected from among the ten heads of the great departments," I suggested.

"Precisely, but the heads of departments are not eligible to the presidency till they have been a certain number of years out of office. It is rarely that a man passes through all the grades to the headship of a department much before he is forty, and at the end of a five years' term he is usually forty-five. If more, he still serves through his term, and if less, he is nevertheless discharged from the industrial army at its termination. It would not do for him to return to the ranks. The interval before he is a candidate for the presidency is intended to give time for him to recognize fully that he has returned into the general mass of the nation, and is identified with it rather than with the industrial army. Moreover, it is expected that he will employ this period in studying the general condition of the army, instead of that of the special group of guilds of which he was the head. From among the former heads of departments who may be eligible at the time, the President is elected by vote of all the men of the nation who are connected with the industrial army."

"The army is not allowed to vote for the President?"

"Certainly not. That would be perilous to its discipline, which it is the business of the President to maintain as the representative of the nation at large. His right hand for this purpose is the inspectorate, a highly important department of our system; to the inspectorate come all complaints or information as to defects in goods, insolence or inefficiency of officials, or dereliction of any sort in the public service. The inspectorate, however, does not wait for complaints. Not only is it on the alert to catch and sift every rumor of a fault in the service, but it is its business, by systematic and constant oversight and inspection of every branch of th army, to find out what is going wrong before anybody else does. The President is usually not far from fifty when elected, and serves five years, forming an honorable exception to the rule of retirement at forty-five. At the end of his term of office, a national Congress is called to receive his report and approve or condemn it. If it is approved, Congress usually elects him to represent the nation for five years more in the international council. Congress, I should also say, passes on the reports of the outgoing heads of departments, and a disapproval renders any one of them ineligible for President. But it is rare, indeed, that the nation has occasion for other sentiments than those of gratitude toward its high officers. As to their ability, to have risen from the ranks, by tests so various and severe, to their positions, is proof in itself of extraordinary qualities, while as to faithfulness, our social system leaves them absolutely without any other motive than that of winning the esteem of their fellow citizens. Corruption is impossible in a society where there is neither poverty to be bribed nor wealth to bribe, while as to demagoguery or intrigue for office, the conditions of promotion render them out of the question."

"One point I do not quite understand," I said. "Are the members of the liberal professions eligible to the presidency? And if so, how are they ranked with those who pursue the industries proper?"

"They have no ranking with them," replied Doctor Leete. "The members of the technical professions, such as engineers and architects, have a ranking with the constructive guilds; but the members of the liberal professions, the doctors and teachers, as well as the artists and men of letters who obtain remissions of industrial service, do not belong to the industrial army. On this ground they vote for the President, but are not eligible to his office. One of its main duties being the control and discipline of the industrial army, it is essential that the President should have passed through all its grades to understand his business."

"That is reasonable," I said, "but if the doctors and teachers do not know enough of industry to be President, neither, I should think, can the President know enough of medicine and education to control those departments."

"No more does he," was the reply. "Except in the general way that he is responsible for the enforcement of the laws as to all classes, the President has nothing to do with the faculties of medicine and education, which are controlled by boards of regents of their own, in which the President is ex-officio chairman, and has the casting vote. These regents, who, of course, are responsible to Congress, are chosen by the honorary members of the guilds of education and medicine, the retired teachers and doctors of the country."

"Do you know," I said, "the method of electing officials by votes of the retired members of the guilds is nothing more than the application on a national scale of the plan of government by alumni, which we used to a slight extent occasionally in the management of our higher educational institutions."

"Did you, indeed?" exclaimed Doctor Leete, with animation. "That is quite new to me, and I fancy will be to most of us, and of much interest as well. There has been great discussion as to the germ of the idea, and we fancied that there was for once something new under the sun. Well! Well! In your higher educational institutions! That is interesting indeed. You must tell me more of that."

"Truly, there is very little more to tell than I have told already," I replied. "If we had the germ of your idea, it was but as a germ."

•XVIII•

THAT EVENING I SAT UP FOR SOME TIME AFTER THE LADIES had retired, talking with Doctor Leete about the effect of the plan of exempting men from further service to the nation after the age of forty-five, a point brought up by his account of the part taken by the retired citizens in the government.

"At forty-five," said I, "a man still has ten years of good manual labor in him, and twice ten years of good intellectual service. To be superannuated at that age and laid on the shelf must be regarded rather as a hardship than a favor by men of energetic dispositions."

"My dear Mr. West," exclaimed Doctor Leete, beaming upon me, "you cannot have any idea of the piquancy your nineteenth-century ideas have for us of this day, the rare quaintness of their effect. Know; 0 child of another race and yet the same, that the labor we have to render as our part in securing for the nation the means of a comfortable physical existence is by no means regarded as the most important, the most interesting, or the most dignified employment of our powers. We look upon it as a necessary duty to be discharged before we can fully devote ourselves to the higher exercise of our faculties, the intellectual and spiritual enjoyments and pursuits which alone mean life. Everything possible is indeed done by the distribution of burdens, and by all manner of special attractions and incentives to relieve our labor of irksomeness, and, except in a comparative sense, is not usually irksome, and is often inspiring. But it is not our labor, but the higher and larger activities which the performance of our task will leave us free to enter upon, that are considered the main business of existence.

"Of course not all, nor the majority, have those scientific, artistic, literary, or scholarly interests which make leisure the one thing valuable to their possessors. Many look upon the last half of life chiefly as a period for enjoyment of other sorts; for travel, for social relaxation in the company of their lifetime friends; a time for the cultivation of all manner of personal idiosyncrasies and special tastes, and the pursuit of every imaginable form of recreation; in a word, a time for the leisurely and unperturbed appreciation of the good things of the world which they have helped to create. But whatever the differences between our individual tastes as to the use we shall put our leisure to, we all agree in looking forward to the date of our discharge as the time we shall first enter upon the full enjoyment of our birthright, the period when we shall first really attain our majority and become enfranchised from discipline and control, with the fee of our lives vested in ourselves. As eager boys in your day anticipated twenty-one, so men nowadays look forward to forty-five. At twenty-one we become men, but at forty-five we renew youth. Middle age and what you would have called old age are considered, rather than youth, the enviable time of life. Thanks to the better conditions of existence nowadays, and above all the freedom of everyone from care, old age approaches many years later and has an aspect far more benign than in past times. Persons of average constitution usually live to eighty-five or ninety, and at forty-five we are physically and mentally younger. I fancy, than you were at thirty-five. It is a strange reflection that at forty-five, when we are just entering upon the most enjoyable period of life, you already began to think of growing old and to look backward. With you it was the forenoon, with us it is the afternoon, which is the brighter half of life."

After this I remember that our talk branched into the subject of popular sports and recreations at the present time as compared with those of the nineteenth century.

"In one respect," said Doctor Leete, "there is a marked difference. The professional sportsmen, which were such a curious feature of your day, we have nothing answering to, nor are the prizes for which our athletes contend money prizes, as with you. Our contests are always for glory only. The generous rivalry existing between the various guilds, and the loyalty of each worker to his own, afford a constant stimulation to all sorts of games and matches by sea and land, in which the young men take scarcely more interest than the honorary guildsmen who have served their time. The guild yacht races off Marblehead take place next week, and you will be able to judge for yourself of the popular enthusiasm which such events nowadays call out as compared with your day. The demand for panem et circenses preferred by the Roman popular is recognized nowadays as a wholly reasonable one. If bread is the first necessity of life, recreation is a close second, and the nation caters for both. Americans of the nineteenth century were as unfortunate in lacking an adequate provision for the one sort of need as for the other. Even if the people of that period had enjoyed larger leisure, they would, I fancy, have often been at a loss how to pass it agreeably. We are never in that predicament."

•XIX•

IN THE COURSE OF AN EARLY MORNING CONSTITUTIONAL I visited Charleston.

Among the changes, too numerous to attempt to indicate, which mark the lapse of a century in that quarter, I particularly noted the total disappearance of the old state prison.

"That went before my day, but I remember hearing about it," said Doctor Leete, when I alluded to the fact at the breakfast table. "We have no jails nowadays. All cases of atavism are treated in the hospitals."

"Of atavism!" I exclaimed, staring.

"Why, yes," replied Doctor Leete. "The idea of dealing punitively with those unfortunates was given up at least fifty years ago, and I think more."

"I don't quite understand you," I said. "Atavism in my day was a word applied to the cases of persons in whom some trait of a remote ancestor recurred in a noticeable manner. Am I to understand that crime is nowadays looked upon as the recurrence of an ancestral trait?" "I beg your pardon," said Doctor Leete with a smile half-humorous, half-deprecating, "but since you have so explicitly asked the question, I am forced to say that the fact is precisely that."

After what I had already learned of the moral contrasts between the nineteenth and the twentieth centuries, it was doubtless absurd in me to begin to develop sensitiveness on the subject, and probably if Doctor Leete had not spoken with that apologetic air and Mrs. Leete and Edith shown a corresponding embarrassment, I should not have flushed, as I was conscious I did.

"I was not in much danger of being vain of my generation before," I said, "but, really—"

"This is your generation, Mr. West," interposed Edith. "It is the one in which you are living, you know, and it is only because we are alive now that we call it ours."

"Thank you. I will try to think of it so," I said, and as my eyes met hers their expression quite cured my senseless sensitiveness. "After all," I said, with a laugh, "I was brought up a Calvinist, and ought not to be startled to hear crime spoken of as an ancestral trait."

"In point of fact," said Doctor Leete, "our use of the word is no reflection at all on your generation, if, begging Edith's pardon, we may call it yours, so far as seeming to imply that we think ourselves, apart from our circumstances, better than you were. In your day, fully nineteen-twentieths of the crime, using the word broadly to include all sorts of misdemeanors, resulted from the inequality in the possessions of individuals. Want tempted the poor; lust of greater gains, or the desire to preserve former gains, tempted the well-to-do. Directly or indirectly, the desire for money, which then meant every good thing, was the motive of all this crime, the taproot of a vast poison growth, which the machinery of law, courts and police could barely prevent from choking your civilization outright. When we made the nation the sole trustee of the wealth of the people, and guaranteed to all abundant maintenance, on the one hand abolishing want, and on the other checking the accumulation of riches, we cut this root, and the poison tree that overshadowed your society withered, like Jonah's gourd, in a day. As for the comparatively small class of violent crimes against persons, unconnected with any idea of gain, they were almost wholly confined, even in your day, to the ignorant and bestial; and in these days, when education and good manners are not the monopoly of a few, but universal, such atrocities are scarcely ever heard of. You now see why the word 'atavism' is used for crime. It is because nearly all forms of crime known to you are motiveless now, and when they appear can only be explained as the outcropping of ancestral traits. You used to call persons who stole, evidently without any rational motive, kleptomaniacs, and when the case was clear, deemed it absurd to punish them as thieves. Your attitude toward the genuine kleptomaniac is precisely ours toward the victim of atavism, an attitude of compassion and firm but gentle restraint."

"Your courts must have an easy time of it," I observed. "With no private property to speak of, no disputes between citizens over business relations, no real estate to divide or debts to collect, there must be absolutely no civil business at all for them; and with no offenses against property, and mighty few of any sort to provide criminal cases, I should think you might almost do without judges and lawyers altogether."

"We do without the lawyers, certainly," was Doctor Leete's reply. "It would not seem reasonable to us, in a case where the only interest of the nation is to find out the truth, that persons should take part in the proceedings who had an acknowledged motive to color it."

"But who defends the accused?"

"If he is a criminal he needs no defense, for he pleads guilty in most instances," replied Doctor Leete. "The plea of the accused is not a mere formality with us, as with you. It is usually the end of the case."

"You don't mean that the man who pleads not guilty is thereupon discharged?"

"No, I do not mean that. He is not accused on light grounds, and if he denies his guilt, must still be tried. But trials are few, for in most cases the guilty man pleads guilty. When he makes a false plea and is clearly proved guilty, his penalty is doubled. Falsehood, is, however, so despised among us that few offenders would lie to save themselves."

"That is the most astounding thing you have yet told me," I exclaimed. "If lying has gone out of fashion, this is indeed the 'new heavens and the new earth wherein dwelleth righteousness,' which the prophet foretold."

"Such is, in fact, the belief of some persons nowadays," was the doctor's answer. "They hold that we have entered upon the millennium, and the theory from their point of view does not lack plausibility. But as to your astonishment at finding that the world has outgrown lying, there is really no ground for it. Falsehood, even in your day, was not common between gentlemen and ladies, social equals. The lie of fear was the refuge of cowardice, and the lie of fraud the device of the cheat. The inequalities of men and the lust of acquisition offered a constant premium on lying at that time. Yet even then, the man who neither feared another nor desired to defraud him scorned falsehood. Because we are now all social equals, and no man either has anything to fear from another or can gain anything by deceiving him, the contempt of falsehood is so universal that it is rarely, as I told you, that even a criminal in other respects will be found willing to lie. When, however, a plea of not guilty is returned, the judge appoints two colleagues to state the opposite sides of the case. How far these men are from being like your hired advocates and prosecutors, determined to acquit or convict, may appear from the fact that unless both agree that the verdict found is just, the case is tried over, while anything like bias in the tone of either of the judges stating the case would be a shocking scandal."

It occurred to me, as Doctor Leete was speaking, that in all his talk I had heard much of the nation and nothing of the state governments. Had the organization of the nation as an industrial unit done away with the states? I asked.

"Necessarily," he replied. "The state governments would have interfered with the control and discipline of the industrial army, which, of course, required to be central and uniform. Even if the state governments had not become inconvenient for other reasons, they were rendered superfluous by the prodigious simplification in the task of government since your day. Almost the sole function of the administration now is that of directing the industries of the country. Most of the purposes for which governments formerly existed no longer remain to be subserved. We have no army or navy, and no military organization. We have no departments of state or treasury, no excise or revenue services, no taxes or tax collectors. The only function proper of government, as known to you, which still remains, is the judiciary and police system. I have already explained to you how simple is our judicial system as compared with your huge and complex machine. Of course the same absence of crime and temptation to it, which makes the duties of judges so light, reduces the number and duties of the police to a minimum."

"But with no state legislatures, and Congress meeting only once in five years, how do you get your legislation done?"

"We have no legislation," replied Doctor Leete, "that is, next to none. It is rarely that Congress, even when it meets, considers any new laws of consequence, and then it only has power to commend them to the following Congress, lest anything be done hastily. If you will consider a moment, Mr. West, you will see that we have nothing to make laws about. The fundamental principles on which our society is founded settle for all time the strifes and misunderstandings which in your day called for legislation.

"Fully ninety-nine hundredths of the laws of that time concerned the definition and protection of private property and the creations of buyers and sellers. There is neither private property, beyond personal belongings, now, nor buying and selling, and therefore the occasion of nearly all the legislation formerly necessary has passed away. Formerly, society was a pyramid posed on its apex. All the gravitations of human nature were constantly tending to topple it over, it could be maintained upright, or rather up wrong (if you will pardon the feeble witticism), by an elaborate system of constantly renewed props and buttresses and guy-ropes in the form of laws. A central Congress and forty state legislatures, turning out some twenty thousand laws a year, could not make new props fats enough to take the place of those which were constantly breaking down or becoming ineffectual through some shifting of the strain. Now society rests on its base, and is in as little need of artificial supports as the everlasting hills."

"But you have at least municipal governments besides the one central authority?"

"Certainly, and they have important and extensive functions in looking out for the public comfort and recreation, and the improvement and embellishment of the villages and cities."

"But having no control over the labor of their people, or means of hiring it, how can they do anything?"

"Every town or city is conceded the right to retain, for its own public works, a certain proportion of the quota of labor its citizens contribute to the nation. This proportion, being assigned it as so much credit, can be applied in any way desired."

The magnificent health of the young people in the schools impressed me strongly. My previous observations, not only of the notable personal endowments of the family of my host, but of the people I had seen in my walks abroad, had already suggested the idea that there must have been something like a general improvement in the physical standard of the race since my day, and now, as I compared these stalwart young men and fresh, vigorous maidens with the young people I had seen in the schools of the nineteenth century, I was moved to impart my thoughts to Doctor Leete. He listened with great interest to what I said.

"Your testimony on this point," he declared, "is invaluable. We believe that there has been such an improvement as you speak of, but of course it could only be a matter of theory with us. It is an incident of your unique position that you alone in the world of today can speak with authority on this point. Your opinion, when you state it publicly, will, I assure you, make a profound sensation. For the rest it would be strange, certainly, if the race did not show an improvement. In your day, riches debauched one class with idleness of mind and body, while poverty sapped the vitality of the masses by overwork, bad food, and pestilent homes. The labor required of children, and the burdens laid on women, enfeebled the very springs of life. Instead of these maleficent circumstances, all now enjoy the most favorable conditions of physical life; the young are carefully nurtured and studiously cared for; the labor which is required of all is limited to the period of greatest bodily vigor, and is never excessive; care for one's self and one's family, anxiety as to livelihood, the strain of a ceaseless battle for life-all these influences, which once did so much to wreck the minds and bodies of men and women, are known no more. Certainly, an improvement of the species ought to follow such a change. In certain specific respects we know, indeed, that the improvement has taken place. Insanity, for instance, which in the nineteenth century was so terribly common a product of your insane mode of life, has almost disappeared, with its alternative, suicide."

XXII •

WE HAD MADE AN APPOINTMENT TO MEET THE LADIES AT the dining hall for dinner, after which, having some engagement, they left us sitting at table there, discussing our wine and cigars with a multitude of other matters.

"Doctor," said I, in the course of our talk, "morally speaking, your social system is one which I should be insensate not to admire in comparison with any previously in vogue in the world, and especially with that of my own most unhappy century. If I were to fall into a mesmeric sleep tonight as lasting as that other, and meanwhile the course of time were to take a turn backward instead of forward, and I were to wake up again in the nineteenth century, when I had told my friends what I had seen, they would every one admit that your world was a paradise of order, equity, and felicity. But they were a very practical people, my contemporaries, and after expressing their admiration for the moral beauty and material splendor of the system, they would presently begin to cipher and ask how you got the money to make everybody so happy; for certainly, to support the whole nation at a rate of comfort, and even luxury, such as I see around me, must involve vastly greater wealth than the nation produced in my day. Now, while I could explain to them pretty nearly everything else of the main features of your system, I should quite fail to answer this question, and failing there, they would tell me, for they were very close cipherers, that I had been dreaming; nor would they ever believe anything else. In my day, I know that the total annual product of the nation, although it might have been divided with absolute equality, would not have come to more than three or four hundred dollars per head, not very much more than enough to supply the necessities of life with few or any of its comforts. How is it that you have so much more?"

"That is a very pertinent question, Mr. West," replied Doctor Leete, "and I should not blame your friends, in the case you supposed, if they declared your story all moonshine, failing a satisfactory reply to it. It is a question which I cannot answer exhaustively at any one sitting, and as for the exact statistics to bear out my general statements, l shall have to refer you for them to books in my library, but it would certainly be a pity to leave you to be put to confusion by your old acquaintances, in case of the contingency you speak of, for lack of a few suggestions.

"Let us begin with a number of small items wherein we economize wealth as compared with you. We have no national, state, county, or municipal debts, or payments on their account. We have no sort of military or naval expenditures for men or materials, no army, navy, or militia. We have no revenue service, no swarm of tax assessors and collectors. As regards our judiciary, police, sheriffs, and jailers, the force which Massachusetts alone kept on foot in your day far more than suffices for the nation now. We have no criminal class preying upon the wealth of society as you had. The number of persons, more or less absolutely lost to the working force through physical disability, or the lame, sick, and debilitated, which constituted such a burden on the able-bodied in your day, now that all live under conditions of health and comfort, has shrunk to scarcely perceptible proportions, and with every generation is becoming more completely eliminated.

"Another item wherein we save is the disuse of money and the thousand occupations connected with financial operations of all sorts, whereby an army of men was formerly taken away from useful employments. Also consider that the waste of the very rich in your day on inordinate personal luxury has ceased, though, indeed, this item might easily be overestimated. Again, consider that there are no idlers now, rich or poor—no drones.

"A very important cause of former poverty was the vast waste of labor and materials which resulted from domestic washing and cooking, and the performing separately of innumerable other tasks to which we apply the cooperative plan.

"A larger economy than any of these-yes, of all together-is effected by the organization of our distributing system, by which the work done once by the merchants, traders, storekeepers, with their various grades of jobbers, wholesalers, retailers, agents, commercial travelers, and middlemen of all sorts, with an excessive waste of energy in needless transportation and interminable handlings, is performed by one-tenth the number of hands and an unnecessary tum of not one wheel. Something of what our distributing system is like you know. Our statisticians calculate that one-eightieth part of our workers suffices for all the processes of distribution which in your day required one-eighth of the population, so much being withdrawn from the force engaged in productive labor."

"I begin to see," I said, "where you get your greater wealth."

"I beg your pardon," replied Doctor Leete, "but you scarcely do as yet. The economies I have mentioned thus far, in the aggregate, considering the labor they would save directly and indirectly through saving of material, might possibly be equivalent to the addition to your annual production of wealth of one-half its former total. These items are however, scarcely worth mentioning in comparison with other prodigious wastes, now saved, which resulted inevitably from leaving the industries of the nation to private enterprise. However great the economies your contemporaries might have devised in the consumption of products, and however marvelous the progress of mechanical invention, they could never have raised themselves out of the slough of poverty so long as they held to that system.

One's worst enemies were necessarily those of his own trade, for, under your plan of making private profit the motive of production, a scarcity of the article he produced was what each particular producer desired. It was for his interest that no more of it should be produced than he himself could produce. To secure this consummation as far as circumstances permitted, by killing off and discouraging those engaged in his line of industry, was his constant effort. When he had killed off all he could, his policy was to combine with those he could not kill, and convert their mutual warfare into a warfare upon the public at large by cornering the market, as I believe you used to call it, and putting up prices to the highest point people would stand before going without the goods. The daydream of the nineteenth-century producer was to gain absolute control of the supply of some necessity of life, so that he might keep the public at the verge of starvation, and always command famine prices for what he supplied. This, Mr. West, is what was called in the nineteenth century a system of production. I will leave it to you if it does not seem, in some of its aspects, a great deal more like a system for preventing production. Some time when we have plenty of leisure I am going to ask you to sit down with me and try to make me comprehend, as I never yet could, though I have studied the matter a great deal, how such shrewd fellows as your contemporaries appear to have been in many respects ever came to entrust the business of providing for the community to a class whose interest it was to starve it. I assure you that the wonder with us is, not that the world did not get rich under such a system, but that it did not perish outright from want. This wonder increases as we go on to consider some of the other prodigious wastes that characterized it.

"Apart from the waste of labor and capital by misdirected industry, and that from the constant bloodletting of your industrial warfare, your system was liable to periodical convulsions, overwhelming alike the wise and unwise, the successful cutthroat as well as his victim. I refer to the business crises at intervals of five to ten years, which wrecked the industries of the nation, prostrating all weak enterprises and crippling the strongest, and were followed by long periods, often of many years, of so-called dull times, during which the capitalists slowly regathered their dissipated strength while the laboring classes starved and rioted. Then would ensue another brief season of prosperity, followed in turn by another crisis and the ensuing years of exhaustion. As commerce developed, making the nations mutually dependent, these crises became worldwide, while the obstinacy of the ensuing state of collapse increased with the area affected by the convulsions, and the consequent lack of rallying centers. In proportion as the industries of the world multiplied and became complex, and the volume of capital involved was increased, these business cataclysms became more frequent, till, in the latter part of the nineteenth century, there were two years of bad times to one of good, and the system of industry, never before so extended or so imposing, seemed in danger of collapsing by its own weight. After endless discussions, your economists appear by that time to have settled down to the despairing conclusion that there was no more possibility of preventing or controlling these crises than if they had been droughts or hurricanes. It only remained to endure them as necessary evils, and when they had passed over to build up again the shattered structure of industry, as dwellers in an earthquake country keep on rebuilding their cities on the same site.

"So far as considering the causes of the trouble inherent in their industrial system, your contemporaries were certainly correct. They were in its very basis, and must needs become more and more maleficent as the business fabric grew in size and complexity. One of these causes was the lack of any common control of the different industries, and the consequent impossibility of their orderly and coordinate development. It inevitably resulted from this lack that they were continually getting out of step with one another and out of relation with the demand.

"Of the latter there was no criterion such as organized distribution gives us, and the first notice that it had been exceeded in any group of industries was a crash of prices, bankruptcy of producers, stoppage of production, reduction of wages, or discharge of workmen. This process was constantly going on in many industries, even in what were called good times, but a crisis took place only when the industries affected were extensive. The markets then were glutted with goods, of which nobody wanted beyond a sufficiency at any price. The wages and profits of those making the glutted classes of goods being reduced or wholly stopped, their purchasing power as consumers of other classes of goods, of which there was no natural glut, was taken away, and, as a consequence, goods of which there was no natural glut became artificially glutted, till their prices also were broken down, and their makers thrown out of work and deprived of income. The crisis was by this time fairly under way, and nothing could check it till a nation's ransom had been wasted.

"A cause, also inherent in your system, which often produced and always terribly aggravated crises, was the machinery of money and credit. Money was essential when production was in many private hands, and buying and selling were necessary to secure what one wanted. It was, however, open to the obvious objection of substituting for food, clothing, and other things a merely conventional representative of them. The confusion of mind which this favored, between goods and their representative, led the way to the credit system and its prodigious illusions. Already accustomed to accept money for commodities, the people next accepted promises for money, and ceased to look at all behind the representative for the thing represented. Money was a sign of real commodities, but credit was but the sign of a sign. There was a natural limit to gold and silver, that is, money proper, but none to credit, and the result was that the volume of credit, that is, the promises of money, ceased to bear any ascertainable proportion to the money, still less to the commodities, actually in existence. Under such a system, frequent and periodical crises were necessitated by a law as absolute as that which brings to the ground a structure overhanging its center of gravity. It was one of your fictions that the government and the banks authorized by it alone issued money; but everybody who gave a dollar's credit issued money to that extent, which was as good as any to swell the circulation till the next crisis. The great extension of the credit system was a characteristic of the latter part of the nineteenth-century, and accounts largely for the almost incessant business crises which marked that period. Perilous as credit was, you could not dispense with its use, for, lacking any national or other public organization of the capital of the country, it was the only means you had for concentrating and directing it upon industrial enterprises. It was in this way a most potent means for exaggerating the chief peril of the private-enterprise system of industry by enabling particular industries to absorb disproportionate amounts of the disposable capital of the country, and thus prepare disaster. Business enterprises were always vastly in debt for advances of credit, both to one another and to the banks and capitalists, and the prompt withdrawal of this credit at the first sign of a crisis was generally the precipitating cause of it.

"It was the misfortune of your contemporaries that they had to cement their business fabric with a material which an accident might at any moment turn into an explosive. They were in the plight of a man building a house with dynamite for mortar, for credit can be compared with nothing else.

"If you would see how needless were these convulsions of business which I have been speaking of, and how entirely they resulted from leaving industry to private and unorganized management, just consider the working of our system. Overproduction in special lines, which was the great hobgoblin of your day, is impossible now, for by the connection between distribution and production supply is geared to demand like an engine to the governor which regulates its speed. Even suppose by an error of judgment an excessive production of some commodity. The consequent slackening or cessation of production in that line throws nobody out of employment. The suspended workers are at once found occupation in some other department of the vast workshop and lose only the time spent in changing, while, as for the glut, the business of the nation is large enough to carry any amount of product manufactured in excess of demand till the latter overtakes it. In such a case of overproduction, as I have supposed, there is not with us, as with you, any complex machinery to get out of order and magnify a thousand times the original mistake. Of course, having not even money, we still less have credit. All estimates deal directly with the real things, the flour, iron, wood, wool, and labor, of which money and credit were for you the very misleading representatives. In our calculations of cost there can be no mistakes. Out of the annual product the amount necessary for the support of the people is taken, and the requisite labor to produce the next year's consumption provided for. The residue of the material and labor represents what can be safely expended in improvements. If the crops are bad, the surplus for that year is less than usual, that is all. Except for slight occasional effects of such natural causes, there are no fluctuations of business, the material prosperity of the nation flows on uninterruptedly from generation to generation, like an ever broadening and deepening river.

"Your business crises, Mr. West," continued the doctor, "like either of the great wastes I mentioned before, were enough, alone, to have kept your noses to the grindstone forever; but I have still to speak of one other great cause of your poverty, and that was the idleness of a great part of your capital and labor. With us it is the business of the administration to keep in constant employment every ounce of available capital and labor in the country. In your day there was no general control of either capital or labor, and a large part of both failed to find employment. 'Capital,' you used to say, 'is naturally timid,' and it would certainly have been reckless if it had not been timid in an epoch when there was a large preponderance of probability that any particular business venture would end in failure. There was no time when, if security could have been guaranteed it, the amount of capital devoted to productive industry could not have been greatly increased. The proportion of it so employed underwent constant extraordinary fluctuations, according to the greater or less feeling of uncertainty as to the stability of the industrial situation, so that the output of the national industries greatly varied in different years. But for the same reason that the amount of capital employed at times of special insecurity was far less than at times of somewhat greater security, a very large proportion was never employed at all, because the hazard of business was always very great in the best, of times.

"It should be also noted that the great amount of capital always seeking employment where tolerable safety could be insured terribly embittered the competition between capitalists when a promising opening presented itself. The idleness of capital, the result of its timidity, of course meant the idleness of labor in corresponding degree. Moreover, every change in the adjustments of business, every slightest alteration in the condition of commerce or manufactures, not to speak of the innumerable business failures that took place yearly, even in the best of times, were constantly throwing a multitude of men out of employment for periods of weeks or months, or even years. A great number of these seekers after employment were constantly traversing the country, becoming in time professional vagabonds, then criminals. 'Give us work!' was the cry of an army of the unemployed at nearly all seasons, and in seasons of dullness in business this army swelled to a host so vast and desperate as to threaten the stability of the government. Could there conceivably be a more conclusive demonstration of the imbecility of the system of private enterprise as a method for enriching a nation than the fact that, in an age of such general poverty and want of everything, capitalists had to throttle one another to find a safe chance to invest their capital and workmen rioted and burned because they could find no work to do?

"Now, Mr. West," continued Doctor Leete, "I want you to bear in mind that these points of which I have been speaking indicate only negatively the advantages of men at that epoch that the only stable elements in human nature, on which a social system could be safely founded, were its worst propensities. They had been taught and believed that greed and self-seeking were all that held mankind together, and that all human associations would fall to pieces if anything were done to blunt the edge of these motives or curb their operation. In a word, they believed-even those who longed to believe otherwise-the exact reverse of what seems to us self-evident; they believed, that is, that the antisocial qualities of men, and not their social qualities, were what furnished the cohesive force of society. It seemed reasonable to them that men lived together solely for the purpose of overreaching and oppressing one another, and of being overreached and oppressed, and that while a society that gave full scope to these propensities could stand, there would be little chance for one based on the idea of cooperation for the benefit of all. It seems absurd to expect any one to believe that convictions like these were ever seriously entertained by men; but that they were not only entertained by our great-grandfathers, but were responsible for the long delay in doing away with the ancient order, after a conviction of its intolerable abuses had become general, is as well established as any fact in history can be. Just here you will find the explanation of the profound pessimism of the literature of the last quarter of the nineteenth century, the note of melancholy in its poetry, and the cynicism of its humor.

"Feeling that the condition of the race was unendurable, they had no clear hope of anything better. They believed that the evolution of humanity had resulted in leading it into a cul de sac, and that there was no way of getting forward. The frame of men's minds at this time is strikingly illustrated by treaties which have come down to us, and may even now be consulted in our libraries by the curious, in which laborious arguments are pursued to prove that despite the evil plight of men, life was still, by some slight preponderance of considerations, probably better worth living than leaving. Despising themselves, they despised their Creator. There was a general decay of religious belief. Pale and watery gleams, from skies thickly veiled by doubt and dread, alone lighted up the chaos of earth. That men should doubt Him whose breath is in their nostrils, or dread the hands that molded them, seems to us indeed a pitiable insanity; but we must remember that children who are brave by day have sometimes foolish fears at night. The dawn has come since then. It is very easy to believe in the fatherhood of God in the twentieth century.

"Briefly, as must needs be a discourse of this character, I have adverted to some of the causes which had prepared men's minds for the change from the old to the new order, as well as some causes of the conservatism of despair which for a while held it back after the time was ripe. To wonder at the rapidity with which the change was completed after its possibility was first entertained is to forget the intoxicating effect of hope upon minds long accustomed to despair. The sunburst, after so long and dark a night, must needs have had a dazzling effect. From the moment men allowed themselves to believe that humanity after all had not been meant for a dwarf, that its squat stature was not the measure of its possible growth, but that it stood upon the verge of an avatar of limitless development, the reaction must needs have been overwhelming. It is evident that nothing was able to stand against the enthusiasm which the new faith inspired.

"Poverty with servitude had been the result, for the mass of humanity, of attempting to solve the problem of maintenance from the individual standpoint, but no sooner had the nation become the sole capitalist and employer than not alone did plenty replace poverty, but the last vestige of the serfdom of man to man disappeared from earth. Human slavery, so often vainly scotched, at last was killed. The means of subsistence no longer doled out by men to women, by employer to employed, by rich to poor, was distributed from a common stock as among children at the father's table. It was impossible for a man any longer to use his fellow men as tools for his own profit. His esteem was the only sort of gain he could thenceforth make out of him. There was no more either arrogance or servility in the relations of human beings to one another. For the first time since the Creation every man stood up straight before God. The fear of want and the lust of gain became extinct motives when abundance was assured to all and immoderate possessions made impossible of attainment. There were no more beggars nor almoners. Equity left charity without an occupation. The ten commandments became well-nigh obsolete in a world where there was no temptation to theft, no occasion to lie either for fear or favor, no room for envy where all were equal, and little provocation to violence where men were disarmed of power to injure one another. Humanity's ancient dream of liberty, equality, fraternity, mocked by so many ages, at last was realized.

"As in the old society the generous, the just, the tender-hearted had been placed at a disadvantage by the possession of those qualities, so in the new society the cold-hearted, the greedy, and self-seeking found themselves out of joint with the world. Now that the conditions of life for the first time ceased to operate as a forcing process to develop the brutal qualities of human nature, and the premium which had heretofore encouraged selfishness was not only removed, but placed upon unselfishness, it was for the first time possible to see what unperverted human nature really was like. The depraved tendencies, which had previously overgrown and obscured the better to so large an extent, now withered like cellar fungi in the open air, and the nobler qualities showed a sudden luxuriance which turned cynics into panegyrists and for the first time in human history tempted mankind to fall in love with itself. Soon was fully revealed, what the divines and philosophers of the old world never would have believed, that human nature in its essential qualities is good, not bad, that men by their natural intention and structure are generous, not self-ish, pitiful, not cruel, sympathetic, not arrogant, godlike in aspirations, instinct with divinest impulses of tenderness and self-sacrifice, images of God indeed, not the travesties upon Him they had seemed. The constant pressure, through numberless generations, of conditions of life which might have perverted angels, had not been able to essentially alter the natural nobility of the stock, and these conditions once removed, like a bent tree, it had sprung back to its normal uprightness.

"To put the whole matter in the nutshell of a parable, let me compare humanity in the olden time to a rosebush planted in a swamp, watered with black bog water, breathing miasmatic fogs by day, and chilled with poison dews at night. Innumerable generations of gardeners had done their best to make it bloom, but beyond an occasional half-opened bud with a worm at the heart, their efforts had been unsuccessful. Many, indeed, claimed that the bush was no rosebush at all, but a noxious shrub fit only to be uprooted and burned. The gardeners, for the most part, however, held that the bush belonged to the rose family, but had some ineradicable taint about it, which prevented the buds from coming out, and accounted for its generally sickly condition. There were a few, indeed, who maintained that the stock was good enough, that the trouble was in the bog, and that under more favorable conditions the plant might be expected to do better. But these persons were not regular gardeners, and being condemned by the latter as mere theorists and daydreamers, were, for the most part, so regarded by the people. Moreover, urged some eminent moral philosophers, even conceding for the sake of the argument that the bush might possibly do better elsewhere, it was a more valuable discipline for the buds to try to bloom in a bog than it would be under more favorable conditions. The buds that succeeded in opening might indeed be very rare, and the flowers pale and scentless, but they represented far more moral effort than if they had bloomed spontaneously in a garden.

"The regular gardeners and the moral philosophers had their way. The bush remained rooted in the bog, and the old course of treatment went on. Continually new varieties of forcing mixtures were applied to the roots, and more recipes than could be numbered, each declared by its advocates the best and only suitable preparation, were used to kill the vermin and remove the mildew. This went on a very long time. Occasionally someone claimed to observe a slight improvement in the appearance of the bush, but there were quite as many who declared that it did not look so well as it used to. On the whole there could not be said to be any marked change. Finally, during a period of general despondency as to the prospects of the bush where it was, the idea of transplanting it was again mooted, and this time found favor. 'Let us try it,' was the general voice. 'Perhaps it may thrive better elsewhere, and here it is certainly doubtful if it be worth cultivating longer.' So it came about that the rosebush of humanity was transplanted, and set in sweet, warm, dry earth, where the sun bathed it, the stars wooed it, and the south wind caressed it. Then it appeared that it was indeed a rosebush. The vermin and the mildew disappeared, and the bush was covered with most beautiful red roses, whose fragrance filled the world.

"It is a pledge of the destiny appointed for us that the Creator has set in our hearts an infinite standard of achievement, judged by which our past attainments seem always insignificant, and the goal never nearer. Had our forefathers conceived a state of society in which men should live together like brethren dwelling in unity, without strife or envying, violence or overreaching, and where, at the price of a degree of labor not greater than health demands, in their chosen occupations, they should be wholly freed from care for the morrow and left with no more concern for their livelihood than trees which are watered by unfailing streams-had they conceived such a condition, I say, it would have seemed to them nothing less than paradise. They would have confounded it with their idea of heaven, nor dreamed that there could possibly lie further beyond anything to be desired or striven for.

"But how is it with us who stand on this height which they gazed up to? Already we have well-nigh forgotten, except when it is especially called to our minds by some occasion like the present, that it was not always with men as it is now. It is a strain on our imaginations to conceive the social arrangements of our immediate ancestors. We find them grotesque. The solution of the problem of physical maintenance so as to banish care and crime, so far from seeming to us an ultimate attainment, appears but as a preliminary to anything like real human progress. We have but relieved ourselves of an impertinent and needless harassment which hindered our ancestors from undertaking the real ends of existence. We are merely stripped for the race; no more. We are like a child which has just learned to stand upright and walk. It is a great event, from the child's point of view, when he first walks. Perhaps he fancies that there can be little beyond that achievement, but a year later he has forgotten that he could not always walk. His horizon did but widen when he rose, and enlarge as he moved. A great event indeed, in one sense, was his first step, but only as a beginning, not as the end. His true career was but then first entered on. The enfranchisement of humanity in the last century, from mental and physical absorption in working and scheming for the mere bodily necessities, may be regarded as a species of second birth of the race, without which its first birth to an existence that was but a burden would forever have remained unjustified, but whereby it is now abundantly vindicated. Since then, humanity has entered on a new phase of spiritual development, an evolution of higher faculties, the very existence of which in human nature our ancestors scarcely suspected. In place of the dreary hopelessness of the nineteenth century, its profound pessimism as to the future of humanity, the animating idea of the present age is an enthusiastic conception of the opportunities of our earthly existence, and the unbounded possibilities of human nature. The betterment of mankind from generation to generation, physically, mentally, morally, is recognized as the one great object supremely worthy of effort and of sacrifice. We believe the race for the first time to have entered on the realization of God's ideal of it, emd each generation must now be a step upward.

"Do you ask what we look for when unnumbered generations shall have passed away? I answer, the way stretches far before us, but the end is lost in light. For twofold is the return of man to God 'who is our home,' the return of the individual by the way of death, and the return of the race by the fulfillment of the evolution, when the divine secret hidden in the germ shall be perfectly unfolded. With a tear for the dark past, turn we then to the dazzling future, and, veiling our eyes, press forward. The long and weary winter of the race is ended. Its summer has begun. Humanity has burst the chrysalis. The heavens are before it."

Postscript

The Rate of the World's Progress

To the Editor of the Boston Transcript: The Transcript of March 30, 1888, contained a review of *Looking Backward*, in response to which I beg to be allowed a word. The description to which the book is devoted, of the radically new social and industrial institutions and arrangements supposed to be enjoyed by the people of the United States in the twentieth century, is not objected to as depicting a degree of human felicity and moral development necessarily unattainable by the race, provided time enough had been allowed for its evolution from the present chaotic state of society. In failing to allow this, the reviewer thinks that the author has made an absurd mistake, which seriously detracts from the value of the book as a work of realistic imagination. Instead of placing the realization of the ideal social state a scant fifty years ahead, it is suggested that he should have made his figure seventy-five centuries. There is certainly a large discrepancy between seventy-five centuries and fifty years, and if the reviewer is correct in his estimate of the probable rate of human progress, the outlook of the world is decidedly discouraging. But is he right? I think not.

Looking Backward, although in form a fanciful romance, is intended, in all seriousness, as a forecast, in accordance with the principles of evolution, of the next stage in the industrial and social development of humanity, especially in this country; and no part of it is believed by the author to be better supported by the indications of probability than the implied prediction that the dawn of the new era is already near at hand, and that the full day will swiftly follow. Does this seem at first thought incredible, in view of the vastness of the changes presupposed? What is the teaching of history, but that great national transformations, while ages in unnoticed preparation, when once inaugurated, are accomplished with a rapidity and resistless momentum proportioned to their magnitude, not limited by it?

In 1759, when Quebec fell, the might of England in America seemed irresistible, and the vassalage of the colonies assured. Nevertheless, thirty years later, the first President of the American Republic was inaugurated. In 1849, after Novara, Italian prospects appeared as hopeless as at any time since the Middle Ages; yet only fifteen years after, Victor Emmanuel was crowned King of United Italy. In 1864, the fulfillment of the thousand-year dream of German unity was apparently as far off as ever. Seven years later it had been realized, and William had assumed at Versailles the Crown of Barbarossa. In 1832, the original Antislavery Society was formed in Boston by a few so-called visionaries. Thirty-eight years later, in 1870, the society disbanded, its program fully carried out.

These precedents do not, of course, prove that any such industrial and social transformation as is outlined in *Looking Backward* is impending; but they do show that, when the moral and economical conditions for it are ripe, it may be expected to go forward with great rapidity. On no other stage are the scenes shifted with a swiftness so like magic as on the great stage of history when once the hour strikes. The question is not, then, how extensive the scene-shifting must be to set the stage for the new fraternal civilization, but whether there are any special indications that a social transformation is at hand. The causes that have been bringing it ever nearer have been at work from immemorial time. To the stream of tendency setting toward an ultimate realization of a form of society, while vastly more efficient for material prosperity, should also satisfy and not outrage the moral instincts, every sigh of poverty, every tear of pity, every humane impulse, every generous enthusiasm, every true religious feeling, every act by which men have given effect to their mutual sympathy by drawing more closely together for any purpose, have contributed from the beginnings of civilization. That this long stream of influence, ever widening and deepening, is at last about to sweep away the barriers it has so long sapped, is at least one obvious interpretation of the present universal ferment of men's minds as to the imperfections of present social arrangements. Not only are the toilers of the world engaged in something like a worldwide insurrection, but true and humane men and women, of every degree, are in a mood of exasperation, verging on absolute revolt, against social conditions that reduce life to a brutal struggle for existence, mock every dictate of ethics and religion, and render well-nigh futile the efforts of philanthropy.

As an iceberg, floating southward from the frozen North, is gradually undermined by warmer seas, and, become at last unstable, chums the sea to yeast for miles around by the mighty rockings that portend its overturn, so the barbaric industrial and social system, which has come down to us from savage antiquity, undermined by the modern human spirit, riddled by the criticism of economic science, is shaking the world with convulsions that presage its collapse.

All thoughtful men agree that the present aspect of society is portentous of great changes. The only question is, whether they will be for the better or the worse. Those who believe in man's essential nobleness lean to the former view, those who believe in his essential baseness to the latter. For my part, I hold to the former opinion. *Looking Backward* was written in the belief that the Golden Age lies before us and not behind us, and is not far away. Our children will surely see it, and we, too, who are already men and women, if we deserve it by our faith and by our works.

—Edward Bellamy
1888

About the Author

Edmond Dantes Vongehr served in World War II as a volunteer with the Army Air Corps. He spent over thirty months flying in a B-24 Liberator bomber. He has been a self-employed insurance agent and broker for over thirty years. Along with twenty years' experience as a real estate broker, land developer, mobile home dealer, and world traveler, his sidelines of activity were gold mining and prospecting in New Zealand, Australia, and Alaska.

www.ingramcontent.com/pod-product-compliance
Lightning Source LLC
Chambersburg PA
CBHW051042250726
48656CB00001B/101